# Mafeking!
## The story of a siege

*Malcolm Flower-Smith*
*Edmund Yorke*

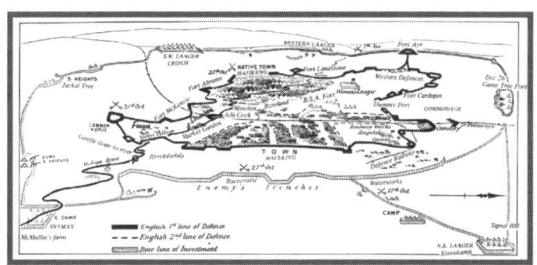

# Mafeking!
## The story of a siege

COVOS-DAY

Published by Covos-Day Books, 2000
Oak Tree House, Tamarisk Avenue,
P.O. Box 6996, Weltevredenpark 1715, South Africa

Copyright ©Edmund Yorke and Malcolm Flower-Smith, 2000

Cover design by JANT Design
Design and origination by JANT Design, Centurion, South Africa
email: j.design@mweb.co.za

Printed and bound by CTP Book Printers (Pty) Ltd

All rights reserved. No part of this publication may be reproduced, stored, manipulated in any retrieval system, or transmitted in any mechanical, electronic or digital form or by any other means, without the prior written authority of the publishers. Any person who engages in any unauthorized activity in relation to this publication shall be liable to criminal prosecution and claims for civil and criminal damages.

ISBN 0-620-25251-0

*To the memory
of all who died
in the Anglo-Boer War*

## About the authors

**Malcolm Flower-Smith**

Malcolm Flower-Smith joined the Northern Rhodesia Police in 1959 on leaving the Royal Navy. He served in Northern Rhodesia until Zambian independence in 1964, when he and his wife returned to Britain. After studying for a degree he was commissioned into the Royal Army Educational Corps, serving for 23 years until retiring from the Army in 1993. He developed an interest in military history whilst serving on the staff of the Royal Military Academy, Sandhurst. His main interests, until now, have been with the development of small arms and their deployment on the battlefields of the 15th and 16th centuries, and the organization of the Elizabethan militia to meet the Armada threat. He has published articles on these topics and in addition edited the British Army's house magazine, *British Army Review*, in 1991 – 92. He is married with two grown-up sons.

**Edmund Yorke**

Dr Edmund Yorke is a Senior Lecturer in Defence and International Affairs at the Royal Military Academy, Sandhurst. He was born in Romsey, Hampshire in 1954. Since completing his first two BA and MA degrees at Reading and London Universities he has specialized in British Empire and Commonwealth political and military affairs. Dr Yorke's doctoral studies at the University of Cambridge focused upon Northern Rhodesia during World War I and his subsequent articles and books have ranged from colonial war studies (notably the Anglo-Zulu War of 1879) to contemporary African peacekeeping. His most recent publications include contributory chapters to *Diplomacy of the Highest Order: Post-war International Summitry* (Macmillan 1995), and co-editorship of *The New South Africa: Prospects for Domestic and International Security* (Macmillan 1998). He lives in Crowthorne, Surrey.

# Authors' note and acknowledgements

The main inspiration for this book arose two years ago in November 1997, when retired army officer Malcolm Flower-Smith, holidaying in South Africa, was presented with an unpublished manuscript compiled by the late Audrey Renew. She, for many years, had been the curator of the Mafikeng (as Mafeking is now spelt) museum and archives. Her manuscript, largely based on the diary of Mr Algie, the Town Clerk but including other sources, was the key catalyst for this centenary reappraisal of both the Siege and Lord Baden-Powell's conduct of it. On his return to the Royal Military Academy, Sandhurst, Malcolm elicited the collaboration of Dr Edmund Yorke, a Southern African specialist who subsequently became a co-author.

Algie's diary comprised one of a plethora of Siege memoirs, many of which were published during the war or in the decade immediately after the Anglo-Boer War. The most detailed record was provided by war correspondents Major F. D. Baillie's *Mafeking: a Diary of the Siege* (1900), and A. Hamilton's *The Siege of Mafeking* (1900) and these have constituted a major source for this work. By contrast J. E. Neilly's *Besieged with B.P.* (1900), took an unusually radical and more critical view of Baden-Powell's handling of the Siege. The memories of Lady Wilson's *South African Memories* and Sir Alexander Godley's *Life of an Irish Soldier London* (1939), comprise less voluminous but nevertheless important vignettes of life under Siege. Nurse Craufurd's articled recollections, *A Nurse's Diary in besieged Mafeking* (1900), fill an important gap in assessing the medical condition of the garrison.

Two more recently published primary sources have added to the wealth of existing archive material—J. F. Midgley's *Petticoat in Mafeking* (1974), recording, Ada Cock's diaries, reinforces Lady Wilson's specifically female appreciation of the Siege, while Edward Ross's *Diary of the Siege of Mafeking* (1980), is a still neglected, critical account that has been widely utilized by the authors of this book. Finally, the sole, existing written record of the African perspective of the Siege, namely S. T. Plaatje's *Mafeking Diary* (1973), remains a crucial adjunct to the many contemporary European diary sources.

Of the many unpublished primary sources, Baden-Powell's own Staff diaries, remain the richest source if one is to identify the motivation behind his Siege policies and the overall view "from the top". The diaries of another leading player, Mr Bell the Civil Commissioner, have yet to be published and are currently housed in Rhodes University Library at Grahamstown, South Africa. The Public Record Office in Kew, London, and the Scout Association Archives in South Kensington, also provide a wealth of ancillary material to the Siege of Mafeking, the former including important War Office and Foreign Office despatches and correspondence.

Since Lord Baden-Powell's death in 1941 the story of this epic Siege, his leadership role and the overall military significance of the Siege has, however, been the focus of considerable controversy. While the major biographies (E. E. Reynolds's *Baden-Powell; a Biography* (1942), and W. Hillcourt and Olave Baden-Powell's, *Baden-Powell; Two Lives of a Hero* (1947), and D. Grinnel-Milnes's *Baden-Powell at Mafeking* (1957)) were largely uncritical in their discussions of his defence of the town, the late 1960s triggered off a barrage of critical books and articles. Brian Gardner's 1966 work, *Mafeking: a Victorian Legend*, for instance, denigrated Baden-Powell's overall leadership, arguing that his role was grossly exaggerated, that he allowed himself to become entrapped at Mafeking, and that the Siege was more a reflection of his unbridled egotism. His implied criticism of Baden-Powell's rationing policy, is continued in M. Rosenthal's work *The Character Factory* (1986), which highlights Baden-Powell's alleged deliberate neglect of the African population of Mafeking. Rosenthal also casts doubt on Baden-Powell's sexuality by highlighting his close relationship with a 13th Hussar officer, Captain Kenneth McLaren. In his magisterial and scholarly account, *The Boer War* (1979), Thomas Pakenham lays a more detailed and serious charge attacking Baden-Powell's role in the defence of Mafeking. Pakenham claims that not only had the 'white garrison taken part of the rations of the black garrison' but 'part of the black garrison was... given the choice of starving to death in the town or running the gauntlet of the Boers' (page 406).

The most detailed riposte to these charges emerges in Tim Jeals's 1989 biography, *Baden-Powell* in which, by close reference to documentary sources deployed or even mis-deployed (!) by Gardner, Rosenthal and Pakenham he, as we shall see, almost totally refutes such stinging criticism of Baden-Powell's character and actions. On the verge of the millennium another, perhaps the most vitriolic attack on Baden-Powell's role during the Mafeking Siege has emerged—*The Boy: Baden-Powell and the Siege of Mafeking* (1999) by Pat Hopkins and Heather Dugmore. This book has recently received wide press coverage, both in South Africa and in Britain. While rightly highlighting the role of the local Baralong in defending Mafeking, the co-authors have not only reiterated Pakenham's and Rosenthal's charges of deliberate neglect of the African population but, have described his alleged "leave or starve policy at Mafeking" as, in Mr Hopkins's words, 'crime against humanity for which he deserves to be re-appraised as a war criminal'. (*Daily Mail*, 12th February 1999).

This centennial study aims to establish a far more balanced view of both the conduct of the Siege and Baden-Powell's leadership role. While, as with many prominent public figures, it is accepted that political and military blunders were made, the authors seek to show that not only was Baden-Powell no more racially prejudiced than the vast majority of his generation, but, that he was the reluctant victim of external military pressures or imperatives outside his control; that he was in fact a formidable military leader; and, that he privately valued the African contribution to the Siege far more than he has hitherto been given credit for. Indeed, a special focus will be made upon the overall black experience of the Siege and, in particular, the economic and military contribution of the loyal African auxiliaries as well as the implications of their consequent highly politicized role for social order and stability during the immediate post Siege period.

The authors would like to pay tribute to the Honourable Mrs Berry Clay CBE, Lord Baden-Powell's last surviving daughter, for not only agreeing to write the foreword to this book but, also for lending key source material including personal copies of his autobiography and his biography by William Hillcourt. We would also like to thank the following ladies for their excellent and unstinting typing support: Elaine Allen, Carole Nightingale, Pauline Medhurst, Rosemary Raggett and Yolande Richardson. Special thanks are also due to Andrew Orgill, Principal Librarian, and Assistant Librarian, Sarah Oliver for their marvellous support in acquiring the source material for this book.

Grateful thanks to the Mafikeng Museum for allowing Rob Milne to photograph some of their exhibits.

We are also very grateful to Priscilla Flower-Smith, Andrew Thom and Michael Ranson for their help and support.

Special thanks go to Rob Milne in South Africa for gathering all the photographic material. And finally, our thanks to the editorial team at Covos-Day Books—Chris Cocks, Martyn Day and Lyn Voigt.

Malcolm Flower-Smith
Edmund Yorke
RMA Sandhurst
Christmas 1999.

# CONTENTS

|  |  | Page |
|---|---|---|
| Foreword by the Hon. Mrs Betty Clay CBE | | xii |
| Chapter 1 | Setting the scene | 1 |
| Chapter 2 | Gentlemen, officers and civilians under arms—the European participants | 10 |
| Chapter 3 | Role of the European ladies and non-European communities | 25 |
| Chapter 4 | The organization of the defence | 38 |
| Chapter 5 | The campaign | 46 |
| Chapter 6 | Early days—October to November 1899 | 70 |
| Chapter 7 | Christmas under siege—December 1899 | 84 |
| Chapter 8 | The ordeal escalates—January to February 1900 | 96 |
| Chapter 9 | The final desperate weeks—March to April 1900 | 114 |
| Chapter 10 | The relief of Mafeking—May 1900 | 135 |
| Conclusion | | 161 |
| Bibliography | | 167 |
| Index | | 170 |

## Foreword

### by The Honorouble Mrs Betty Clay CBE

It is long ago since I last thought about the Siege of Mafeking, and even longer since my father told us as children some of the enthralling stories recounted here in Malcolm Flower-Smith and Edmund Yorke's fascinating book.

They start with a masterly summary of why the British and the Boers clashed into determined warfare, and well-researched descriptions of the military leaders involved, and their later achievements.

My father is included in these, and he used to tell us of one voyage to South Africa: in 1899 when he was on leave in England from India, he was summoned by Lord Wolseley, the Commander in Chief and ordered to go to South Africa to prepare for the Boer War. The conversation went something like this:

Wolseley: Can you sail next Saturday?
B-P: I'm afraid not, sir.
W: Oh? Why not?
B-P: Because there is no ship sailing that day, but the weekly mail-boat sails Friday, so I can go then.

It was surprising to read of the extraordinary mixture of peoples there were trapped in that small isolated spot: there were several different groups of African tribes; a number of individuals including women and children from many other countries. I was filled with admiration to read of their steadfastness in the face of deprivation, shortages, and physical danger. It's certain that they provided inspiration for their menfolk, strengthening their resolve to win through to the end.

The description of the layout of the area makes one realize how difficult it was to prevent it being overwhelmed by a determined and strongly armed enemy; and one can well-understand that "adaptation and making-do was a way of life for those besieged".

Among the reasons the Boers did not make any attack in force was that they were deceived into believing that there were searchlights all round, when the defenders shone their one searchlight from many different positions. The defenders also buried boxes thought to contain mines, some of which were detonated to prove the reality.

It is clear that the people of Mafeking were encouraged to carry out such ruses because my father had got to know many Boer people and their ways, as he wrote later: "I have always had a feeling of sympathy with the Boers and when I was on a joint Commission of Boers and British delegates to Swaziland in 1889, I got to know and understand them, and to recognize the many sterling qualities they possess."

These and similar ruses seem to have deterred the Boers from greater attacks, and Edmond and Malcolm's book gives us well-researched accounts of the terrifying skirmishes that filled the following months, showing how each side achieved varying successes or rebuffs. It was interesting to note how the besieged turned from an atmosphere of excitement at the novelty of being at war to a feeling of "fear" and thence to a sense of fatalism—with each set-back making them more closely linked into a team.

There are many moving accounts of great personal heroism, by people of all races and situations, such as "no more loyal men could possibly be found than the Chiefs of the Baralong nation… and the African runners, scouts and messengers, often carried out at the cost of their own lives—if not, gross maltreatment when captured."

And among those heroes, were the young boys who were the "Cadets", organized by Lord Edward Cecil, whose bold and selfless service became one of the factors that inspired my father to give the Scout Movement to the boys of the world.

Throughout the last few months hunger and the spectre of starvation must have haunted everyone. It is difficult to imagine what utter joy and relief must have been felt by *all* when the Siege was over and the Besiegers could return to rebuild their ruined homes, and the Besieged could start new more useful lives.

And as "the Colonel" summed it up: 'We worked as a well-organized team; we relied on our imagination and resourcefulness to use what materials we had available. Actually, it was all a matter of a great deal of bluff'.

Betty Clay
Pax 3, Elliscombe Park,
Holton, Near Wincanton,
Somerset,
England.
15th January 2000

## Chapter 1

## Setting the scene

**The origins of war**

The Anglo-Boer or South African War of 1899 – 1902 is regarded as the most serious conflict that confronted Britain between the Crimean and the First World War. Although, primarily, it represented a struggle between whites for political power, it was equally, as the second title suggests, a war that eventually necessitated, indeed demanded, the participation of local African communities on a large scale. For both Afrikaner white communities and African polities, in particular, it was to prove a time of great hardship and ultimately great suffering. By the end of the almost three year struggle nearly 7,000 Boer combatants lay dead, and a further 26,000 to 28,000 Boer civilians, mainly women and children had perished in the dreaded British "concentration camps". The latter tragedy left a bitter legacy of Afrikaner hatred for the British that has lingered on to this day. Twenty-two thousand imperial soldiers also died, the majority from disease. The sheer magnitude or scale of the conflict rapidly became evident as up to 50,000 highly mobile Boer commando fighters faced a massive British imperial Army which eventually reached almost half a million men. To this must be added countless Africans who died as innocent civilians or in logistical support roles but, more controversially, as we shall see, as armed auxiliaries for both sides.

The origins of the Anglo-Boer conflict stretched back for at least a century preceding the outbreak of war in October 1899. While the first substantial Dutch settlement in the area occurred in 1652 it was not until the 1790s that Britain first occupied the area for strategic reasons during the Revolutionary and Napoleonic Wars. Serious friction between the primarily agrarian Afrikaner settlers and their British masters only arose after 1814 when the Cape of Good Hope became a permanent British possession. The steady imposition of British taxes incensed Boer farmers but it was two particular events that set the scene for future political and military confrontation. The adoption of English as the official language of the colony in 1828 and the 1833 British Parliamentary Act emancipating slaves throughout the British Empire affronted the fiercely independent Boer farming communities. Boer religious beliefs which rested on strict Calvinism and a perception of African tribal groups as primarily "hewers of wood and drawers of water" reflecting their economic dependence on slave labour, led many to take the drastic action of literally trekking out of the area, thus physically cutting off links with British authority. The Great Trek of 1836, launched deep into the Southern African interior, led to serious armed clashes with interior African groups including the crushing defeat of the Zulu armies at Blood River in 1838, all of which further enhanced the generation of a distinct Afrikaner identity and a deep felt sense of nationhood. It was a short-lived freedom. Britain's reaction to the Great Trek—the annexation of Natal in 1843 and the eventual penetration of the area between the Orange and Vaal rivers, only served to resurrect the tension between the recalcitrant Boer farmers and their former imperial masters.

The recognition by Britain of Boer independence beyond the Vaal and the Orange rivers (Sand River and Bloemfontein Conventions of 1852 and 1854) reflected a revised British government perception of their limited, political and strategic importance. Again however, this proved to be only a brief respite for the scattered Boer communities who increasingly saw themselves as the eternally beleaguered "white tribe of Africa". From the late 1850s onwards pressure to confederate together both the British colonies and these embryonic Afrikaner republics of the Orange Free State and the Transvaal steadily increased if only to secure the region from the continual internal "native wars" and thereby reduce local and imperial expenditure.

Economic events provided the final catalyst to direct military clashes between Briton and Boer. The discovery of diamonds in significant quantities during the 1860s revived British interest in the region and the new imperial interventionism was reflected in Lord Carnarvon's attempts to both confederate and ultimately control the whole region under British sovereignty. The twin British annexations of Basutoland (Lesotho) in 1868 after the Free State–Basuto War and diamond-rich Griqualand West in 1871, reinforced Afrikaner perceptions of British perfidy and imminent domination. In 1877 the bankruptcy of the Transvaal republic itself embroiled in disastrous conflicts with local African tribes, enabled the British to annex this state and further confirm Boer fears.

From 1879 to 1881 military pressures came to the fore as Britain's expansionist frontier policies, rejuvenated under the new South African High Commissioner, Sir Bartle Frere, embroiled Britain in a costly war against the Zulu, the last African obstacle to the grandiose plan of South African confederation. The resultant Pyrrhic victory not only cost the Treasury several hundred million pounds but also led to a series of devastating military blunders as the British forces initially suffered serious defeats notably at the battle of Isandlwana and Intombe Drift. Despite the inevitable final elimination of Zulu power at the battle of Ulundi in July 1879, two years later the discontented Transvaal Boers, emboldened by these apparent British military weaknesses and supported by their Orange Free

State compatriots, rose in revolt. Caught largely by surprise the often-outnumbered British forces in the region suffered a series of setbacks culminating in the humiliating defeat at Majuba Hill in February 1881. To the dismay of many, Gladstone's Liberal Government, appalled at the cost of this unexpected war and embarrassed by its political implications, signed the Pretoria Convention (modified by the London Convention of 1884) which granted the Transvaal a limited form of independence.

The humiliation of Majuba however, combined with the 1886 discovery of rich seams of gold in the Transvaal ensured that the Boer Republics would never escape the vengeful attentions of the British imperial metropole. As strategic fears escalated, particularly following the enhanced interest of Germany in the region, British pressures became more intense than ever before. In the 1890s control of the alleged pro-German Transvaal Government became a burning imperative. The disastrous 1895 Jameson Raid, an attempted armed coup against the Transvaal foolishly supported by Cecil Rhodes, Prime Minister of the Cape, who considered that British capital interests in Johannesburg were too great to be left to the mercies of what was perceived to be an inefficient, corrupt and clearly anti-British Kruger Government, made war a virtual certainty. British hopes now rested upon the issue of the Uitlander franchise. Following the discovery of gold the Transvaal had been flooded by foreign miners, predominantly British and known as "Uitlanders" or outsiders. President Paul Kruger, of the Transvaal, soon realized the direct political threat posed by these white British immigrants and proceeded to refuse the extension of citizenship and the franchise and thereby prevent de facto British control of his country. As pressures from the newly appointed and fervent imperialist, the High Commissioner, Sir Alfred Milner, closely supported in London by Joe Chamberlain, the Colonial Secretary, massively increased in the closing months of 1899, Kruger fearing imminent war and aware of the enervated state of British forces in the region, decided to launch a pre-emptive strike. In October 1899, five months after the failure of the

# Setting the scene

Bloemfontein talks between Kruger and Milner, the Transvaal President delivered an ultimatum requiring Britain to immediately cease all overseas troop reinforcements and movement in the region. Britain predictably refused to comply and war broke out with a rapid invasion of Natal by Boer forces and the encirclement of the key strategic centres of Kimberley, Ladysmith and Mafeking.

## Baden-Powell's party
In the summer of 1899 Colonel Baden-Powell left a meeting in the War Office with the Commander-in-Chief of the British Army, Lord Wolseley, with instructions to lead a small group of regular officers to South Africa. Their mission was to recruit two regiments of irregular mounted troops which on the outbreak of any hostilities were 'to act as bait for the Boers on the western frontier of the Transvaal and Orange Free State to divert as many Boer commandos as possible from the main theatre of operations'[1]. Lord Wolseley, and the Colonial Office, were concerned about the deteriorating relations with President Kruger's Transvaal Republic and wanted to be ready in case war broke out.

Colonel Baden-Powell was a good choice for this task. He was a cavalry officer, late of the 13th Lancers, who had spent much time abroad and had experience of fighting in Africa and India. He had commanded the 5th Dragoons in India. He had developed a keen interest in scouting and reconnaissance and as a result produced a pamphlet *Scouting and Reconnaissance* for the Army. He was known for his lone scouting exploits against the Ashanti in West Africa and the Ndebele in Rhodesia.

It was not uncommon, in those days of the wide flung Empire, for officers to find themselves seconded for special duties, often on their own or in small parties, forced on to their own initiative by circumstances or the difficulties of communications. Colonel Baden-Powell's orders were to recruit two regiments, one in the Protectorate of Bechuanaland at Ramathlabama about 20 miles north of Mafeking and one in Rhodesia at Bulawayo. Lord

Wolseley considered that, on the outbreak of hostilities, Boer commandos would be most likely to sweep out of the Transvaal and Orange Free State striking southwest into Natal and south east into Cape Colony. His intention by setting up the two regiments, one to the west and one to the north-west of the Boer states, was to force the Boers to hold forces back to meet the threat imposed by these British regiments.

Baden-Powell set off at once taking with him, as his Chief Staff Officer (CSO), Major the Lord Edward Cecil[2], Grenadier Guards, fourth son of the Prime Minister, Lord Salisbury and Lieutenant the Honourable Algernon Hanbury-Tracy, Royal Horse Guards (Blues), who was to be his Intelligence Officer (IO). Lady Violet Cecil, Lord Edward's wife travelled with them. The rest of the party travelled a short time later. It seems that Baden-Powell had his small core of about 20 Imperial officers[3] chosen for him, although he does appear to have requested the services of Captain Kenneth McLaren (an old friend and regimental colleague, who was at the time serving as ADC to General Sir Baker Russell, GOC Southern District and former commanding officer of the 13th Hussars), who was ordered to South Africa to join him. The chosen officers, who travelled out together to Cape Town on the *RMS Norman* a few weeks after Baden-Powell included: Colonel C.O.Hore, Lieutenant Colonel Herbert Plumer, Majors Courtney Vyvyan (Buffs) and Alexander Godley (Royal Irish Rangers), Captains Charles FitzClarence (Royal Fusiliers) and Peter Rolt (Yorks and Lancs) and Major Godley, at least, had his wife with him. Altogether there were about 20 Imperial officers[3], most if not all having previous experience of combat in Southern Africa or Rhodesia.

When Colonel Baden-Powell arrived in the Cape he found that the political situation was delicate. Sir Alfred Milner the High Commissioner who had replaced Sir Hercules Robinson (later Lord Rosmead) after the notorious Jameson Raid of 1895, and who was appointed to smooth relations with President Kruger and Pretoria in the aftermath of the raid, was, according to Boer sources[4], spoiling for a fight. Milner was a capable and determined man with a ruthless streak; his views on the Boer Republics were shared by Colonel Hanbury-Williams, his Military Secretary. On the other hand, The GOC, Lieutenant General Sir William Butler, the Senior Military Officer in the Cape disapproved of the aggressive stance being taken by Milner. He had attempted unsuccessfully to warn Joseph Chamberlain, the Colonial Secretary, that Milner's actions and attitudes were leading to war. He disapproved not only of Britain going to war with the Boers but also of the way in which Lord Wolseley saw the campaign opening. In consequence he refused to support or sponsor Baden-Powell's mission.

Baden-Powell was, therefore, thrown back on his own resources and had to raise money on his own initiative for the purchase of horses and stores. This he did. Leaving Major Cecil in Cape Town to sort things out he set off up country accompanied by his Information Officer. Major Lord Cecil eventually had to procure loans of up to a quarter of a million pounds on the security of his father[5]. This lack of support from the local military command, however, was to have its effect in the delay in supplying modern guns and ammunition for Baden-Powell's forces, thus leaving Mafeking to be defended with a collection of old and inadequate artillery and ammunition. Modern guns were dispatched at the last moment but too late. The rail link to Mafeking was cut while they were in transit, and, before they could arrive the Boers captured the guns.

Lord Cecil and his wife eventually set out to follow Baden-Powell but a minor accident to Lady Cecil with treatment from an unshaven, scruffy doctor at Kimberley decided her to return to civilization at Cape Town and await the outcome of events rather than face the tough life of the pioneer. When the *SS Norman* arrived in Cape Town the party aboard discovered that Colonel Baden-Powell had already moved up country and that they were to follow as soon as possible. Sir Alfred Milner was doing what he could to facilitate the mission's needs with the assistance of Colonel Hanbury-Williams. The party quickly set out for the North, Colonel Hore, with Major Godley as his second in command and Captain FitzClarence, together with Lieutenant Colonel Vyvyan, alighting from the train at Mafeking in early August to start raising the Protectorate Regiment whilst Colonel Plumer and the others went on to Bulawayo where the railway ended.

Lieutenant Colonel Hore and party established themselves at Dixon's hotel in Mafeking where they found Lady Sarah Wilson. Lady Sarah was the wife of Captain Gordon Wilson (Blues). She had been accompanying him on a shooting trip in Rhodesia when he had been taken on by Baden-Powell as ADC when Baden-Powell had found him in Bulawayo. Also in the hotel was Major Goold-Adams[6] who was the Resident Commissioner of Bechuanaland.

Colonel Hore and his officers set about recruiting the irregulars of the Protectorate Regiment. The assembling and training of the regiment took place at Ramathlabama, just across the border in Bechuanaland. Meanwhile Colonel Baden-Powell used the time to reconnoitre the western frontier region of the Transvaal to find the best place to act as bait for the Boer forces. His decision fell on Mafeking for two reasons. The first was that the Cape Government had recently announced that a customs duty was shortly to be imposed on all goods being sent to Rhodesia, the consequence of which was that goods of all kinds, including dried and tinned food stuffs, had been stockpiled at Mafeking by traders in anticipation of being shipped north to beat the new tax deadline[7]. In addition he had those military stores[8] that he had been able to obtain stored at Mafeking. It was this concentration of stores that prompted Baden-Powell to seek authorization from the still reluctant Cape Military authorities to move his force into Mafeking at the beginning of October 1899 'to guard', as he put it, these stores. Mafeking, being in Cape Colony, was technically outside Baden-Powell's jurisdiction. The second reason was that setting up a military base at Mafeking had a psychological impact on the Boers as it was from Mafeking that the Jameson Raid of 1895 had been launched into the Transvaal.

## Setting the scene

By 5th October it became apparent that the Boers had begun to concentrate on the Transvaal border close to Mafeking. War was imminent. On the 9th President Kruger issued an ultimatum to the British Government and with its expiry at 5.00 pm, on 11th October 1899, Britain and the Boer Republics were at war.

---

1  Sir Alexander Godley, *Life of an Irish Soldier* (Short title Sir A. Godley).
2  Clearly a good choice, Lord Cecil went on to become a notable colonial administrator in Egypt.
3  Col J. Stirling, *The Colonials in South Africa.*
4  J.C. Smuts, *Jan Christian Smuts* by his son, p. 43-47.
5  D. Grinnel-Milne, *Baden Powell at Mafeking.*
6  Authorities are undecided as to whether *Goold Adams* is hyphenated or not. The Army list shows his name as hyphenated and lists him under Officers seconded for Special Duties. He later became Sir Hamilton Goold-Adams, subsequently Governor of the Orange River Colony, Queensland and High Commissioner in Cyprus.
7  Sir A. Godley.
8  Lady Sarah Wilson makes it plain that the military stores were only sufficient to support the garrison for two weeks and that it was the stores stockpiled by the traders, notably Weil, that permitted the town to hold out for as long as it did.

## Chapter 2

## Gentlemen, officers and civilians under arms

**The European participants**

War at the end of the 19th century had not yet taken on the brutality and totality of post 1914 conflicts. The Boer War was probably the last war in which chivalric and gentlemanly behaviour still played a part, although there is little doubt that the "gentleman" status of some of the colonial officers in the irregular regiments was considered questionable by their British colleagues, as was that of some of the "Johnnie Boer" officers. It is difficult today, at the dawn of the 21st century, to understand the attitudes and lifestyles of our forebears who lived at the turn of the 20th century. In Britain and within British institutions there was an acceptance of one's station in life; the pressures for equality and change in the status quo were in their infancy. The Queen and the Empire had a mystical significance in the minds of all those who went out to fight for them, both the officers and men of the regular Army and the pioneers who came to join the irregular forces. A number of officers combined the privations of both army and pioneer life by being seconded to special duties in command of the British South Africa Police (BSAP) which was set up in 1896 as a result of the repercussions of the Jameson Raid.

Many of those involved in the Boer War had devoted their lives to the hardships of pioneer or army life for the maintenance and expansion of the Queen's dominions.

For officers in the Army at that time advancement to senior rank was primarily through success at the Staff College although there were avenues for promotion by demonstrating efficiency in command and participation in active service. It was through this latter avenue that Colonel Baden-Powell had achieved his rank and position.

## R.S.S. Baden-Powell

This is intended neither as a biography of Baden-Powell nor a complete run down of his military career. However, to gain some understanding of the man and his methods during the siege of Mafeking one needs to know something of his background and career. From the earliest time he had a knack for getting himself noticed by senior officers, and from time to time his talents and abilities were recognized and brought to the attention of Lord Wolseley and Lord Roberts. They remembered him when they were looking for an officer with initiative for a tricky situation.

Robert Stevenson Smyth Baden-Powell ('Baden rhymes with maiden and Powell with noël', he used to say) was born in February 1857. His father was Professor Baden Powell, a retired Oxford professor who died when the boy was three years old, leaving his third wife to bring up her seven children. In memory of her husband, Mrs Powell insisted in changing the family name to incorporate the professor's Christian name. The family surname thus became Baden-Powell. Baden-Powell's Army career began when, on failing to get accepted by Oxford on leaving Charterhouse in 1876, aged 19, he sat and passed the Army entrance exam, coming 3rd for cavalry and 5th for infantry. He chose the cavalry, and as at that time the top six in each arm were exempted attendance at the Royal Military College Sandhurst, he was posted direct to the 13th Hussars.

At the end of October 1876 Sub-lieutenant Baden-Powell left England to join his regiment at Lucknow. During his first two years with the regiment he passed his Lieutenancy examinations in June 1878 with a First Class rating and was promoted to Lieutenant with two years antedate. He seems to have been a singularly self-possessed, popular young man, in great demand for amateur theatricals which were a staple form of garrison entertainment in the cantonments. At the end of two years his health gave out and he was invalided home on sick leave at public expense.

He gradually recovered in the temperate climate of England and was sent on a small arms course and a signalling course at the School of Musketry, Hythe, attaining a First Class pass at the end. This entitled him to an extra 100 rupees per month, a useful salary addition for a young officer of limited means. On his return to India, in the autumn of 1880, Lieutenant Baden-Powell found himself left in charge of the regimental rear party at Lucknow, the main body having moved to Kandahar in Afghanistan. Whilst he was at Lucknow a new doctor and a new young officer, Lieutenant McLaren, reported for duty. Baden-Powell's orders were changed and he, the doctor and McLaren, whose youthful looks won him the nickname[1] "Boy" which stuck with him throughout his military career, were instructed to join the regiment in Afghanistan. Baden-Powell and McLaren struck up a friendship, the two lieutenants sharing a house at Muttra once the regiment returned to India. Their friendship was probably based on their mutual love of polo and pig sticking. We can see from Major Baillie's remarks, in his diary, (after the wrongly reported death of "the Boy") about the loss of McLaren to Hurlingham and the polo field, that McLaren must have been a particularly skilled player, while Baden-Powell's biographer refers to Baden-Powell's skill at this and the sport of pigsticking.

Baden-Powell was always very keen on ensuring his men were well trained and believed that each soldier should be schooled in reconnaissance and scouting. So at Muttra, from his own training notes, he produced and published a pamphlet, *Reconnaissance and Scouting*, to provide other officers with exercises and teaching notes. This was the first of several military pamphlets he was to write[2].

On promotion to Captain, Baden-Powell became adjutant of his regiment, serving for four years in that capacity while the regiment was in India and on its move to Natal, South Africa in 1884, as reinforcements for the First Boer War; although the 13th Hussars saw no action. Baden-Powell was sent out alone on a three week scouting expedition to survey the passes of the Drakensberg by his commanding officer. He disguised the military purpose of his task by claiming to be a newspaper correspondent who was surveying the area to write an article to encourage settlers. This expedition together with other, shooting, expeditions led him to fall in love with Africa.

The 13th Hussars returned to England, to Norwich with a detached squadron in Colchester where Captain Baden-Powell was sent as squadron leader in 1886. He had strong views on training and morale, developing a very efficient squadron over the two years he spent in command. In 1888 his Uncle, General Sir Henry Smyth was appointed General Officer Commanding, South Africa and invited Baden-Powell to be his ADC in the Cape. There was no hesitation; the opportunity to get back to Africa was not to be missed.

He followed his uncle two years later when the General was appointed Governor of Malta. Whilst in Malta, Baden-Powell was appointed Intelligence Officer for the Mediterranean and made a number of undercover trips to Algeria, Turkey and the Balkans on his own. Throughout this period Baden-Powell kept himself very much abreast of military technical developments both at home and abroad, travelling to Germany and Russia whilst on leave in 1886, with his younger brother Baden, also an Army officer, to attend (unofficially) those countries' manoeuvres to discover for himself the effectiveness and rate of fire of the new German machine-gun and the power of the new, vaunted, Russian searchlights.

In late 1895 Major Baden-Powell was appointed to the staff of Sir Francis Scott for the Ashanti Expedition. His task on arrival in the Gold Coast was, with his second in command, Captain Graham, as the only other white officer, to recruit an African levy which was to move ahead of the main body preparing a road and undertaking scouting and pioneering work all the way to Kumasi, the Ashanti capital. On his return to London he was promoted Brevet Lieutenant Colonel. In April 1896, Lieutenant Colonel Baden-Powell found himself appointed Chief of Staff to Sir Frederick Carrington for his expedition against the rebelling tribes of Southern Rhodesia. His services had been expressly requested by Sir Frederick for whom Baden-Powell had worked in Zululand eight years earlier, whilst on loan from Sir Henry Smyth.

This trip to Cape Colony gave him his first glimpse of Mafeking, as at this time it was as far north as the railway reached. From Mafeking the journey to Bulawayo was by "Wells Fargo" style stage coach drawn by ten mules. It took ten days to cover the 560 miles; Sir Frederick, Baden-Powell and two other officers rode inside while three officers' servants and two drivers travelled outside. The rebellious Matabele, retreated into the Matopos hills and Baden-Powell, together with an interpreter and guide, carried out a series of lone scouting expeditions to locate their indunas (headmen). It was during this time that he is first recorded as working with Herbert Plumer who was at this time in command of the special Matabele Relief Force which had been raised in Cape Town.

When now Brevet (full) Colonel Baden Powell returned to the 13th Hussars he found himself in the invidious position of having to return to his substantive rank of Major, junior to his Lieutenant Colonel, Commanding Officer and the senior Major in the regiment. This did not last long and he was offered command of the 5th Dragoon Guards in India, which he took up in 1897. It was while he was on leave from India in London two years later that he was summoned by Lord Wolseley, the Commander-in-Chief, and ordered to Africa to prepare for the Boer War.

### The other officers and the men

At the call to arms for the South African war it is interesting to note that there was no shortage of titled individuals who answered; *Black and White* magazine which was a weekly devoted to the Boer War took pride in announcing that: 'there are 30 Baronets serving in the Army in South Africa', printing a list of them all by name. Still these were a minority of the officers of the forces of the Empire. At the start of the war a number of irregular regiments and corps were raised throughout South Africa, the Imperial Light Horse being one of the best known. It was Major "Karri" Davis of that regiment who was the first person from the relief column to enter Mafeking on 17th May 1900. Karri Davis had been a leader of the Uitlanders in Johannesburg in 1895 at the time of the Jameson Raid and been gaoled for his participation in the revolt. These locally recruited units were not particularly well thought of by the Imperial officers and troops. The term "skallywag", describing the irregular, locally recruited units, appears in more than one contemporary commentary[3], but at Mafeking they conducted themselves bravely and honourably although there was some criticism of the behaviour of the men of the irregular regiments[4] who fought elsewhere in the Boer war.

Mafeking had its share of officers with entries in Debrett. There was Major the Lord Edward Cecil, fourth son of the Prime Minister of the day, Lord Salisbury, without whose influence and assistance when they landed at Cape Town Baden Powell would have had considerable difficulty in carrying out his instructions. Also, Captain Lord Charles Cavendish-Bentinck, who became a squadron leader in the Protectorate Regiment and Captain the honourable Charles FitzClarence, Royal Regiment of Fusiliers[5] and D Squadron Leader in the Protectorate Regiment, whose grandfather, the first Earl Munster, was the son of Mrs Jordan the 18th century actress and the Duke of Clarence (later King William IV). Both Charles Bentinck and Charles FitzClarence distinguished themselves as squadron commanders in the Protectorate Regiment, FitzClarence showing particular dash, leadership and courage in leading a bayonet and sword charge into the Boer trenches, which won him a Victoria Cross. FitzClarence had come out with Baden-Powell's original party whilst Lord Bentinck had joined a little later. There were two other honourables, Captain the honourable Douglas Marsham, British South Africa Police, son of the Earl of Romney, who was killed in the defence of Cannon Kopje on 31st October 1899 and Lieutenant the honourable Algernon Hanbury-Tracy of the Royal Horse Guards who was Baden-Powell's Intelligence Officer.

It is interesting to note that whilst Baden-Powell himself complained that he was given little choice in the selection of the 20 or so officers he was assigned by the War Office to staff his regiments, more than half can be traced to having served in South Africa in earlier campaigns. Thus he was given a selection of men who knew what to expect. Plumer had commanded the Matabeleland Relief Force in 1896, and Major Peter Rolt, his adjutant, who had been in Mashonaland in 1897 together with Major Pilson, Major Bird and Lieutenant Harland, accompanied him now. In Mafeking itself, Baden-Powell had Lieutenant Colonel Courtnay Vyvyan (later Sir Courtnay Vyvyan bt.) who had served in the Zulu War of 1879 and taken part in the battle of Inyezane and been at Eshowe during the investment, the experience of which he, as Base Commandant, no doubt put to use in the preparations he made for the defence of Mafeking. Then there was Major Godley who had served with the Mounted Infantry column sent out from Aldershot in 1897 to help with the pacification of the Mashonaland rebellion.

The Army Lists for this period contain a section devoted to officers detached on Special Duties; one such was Major Goold-Adams who seems to have been employed as a Resident Commissioner for Bechuanaland and who was in Mafeking at the outbreak of the war. Goold-Adams was an officer of the Royal Scots. Promoted Captain on 14th August 1885, he had served with the 1st battalion under Sir Charles Warren in the Bechuanaland Expedition of 1884/85. He continued to serve in

Southern Africa leading the southern Column against Lobengula and the Matebele in the expedition of 1893[6]. By the time of the Mafeking Siege he had been awarded a CMG (Colonial Medal for gallantry). After the siege he continued to have a glittering career, eventually retiring from the Governorship of Cyprus as Sir Hamilton Goold-Adams.

Then there were the officers and troopers seconded to Baden-Powell's forces from the Cape Police and the British South Africa Police. Amongst the latter was Lieutenant Godley, wounded in the final "push" to relieve Mafeking, whose brother was Major Alexander Godley, the second in command of the Protectorate Regiment and in charge of the western defences of the town.

Pictures of the officers in books and magazines of the time show many men whose age would, today, belie their rank. These older men were, on the whole, locally recruited officers, a number of whom were promoted from the ranks during the siege. Corporal Currie, for instance was promoted Lieutenant as reward for his leadership with the Cape Boys in the Brickfields. We know that Major Panzera, the officer in charge of the artillery at Mafeking was 47 years old and that Baden-Powell failed in an attempt to gain for him a Commission in the Royal Artillery on the strength of his good work during the siege. Whether this failure was due to Panzera's age or Royal Artillery prejudice against colonials is not known. Not much is known of the antecedents of the pioneering colonials who came in to join the two locally recruited regiments. However, it seems likely that they were a mixture of "black sheep", adventurers and remittance men. There was for instance Lieutenant Godley, brother to Major Godley on Baden-Powell's staff, who had come out to South Africa in 1896 to find his fortune, had joined the Matebeleland Relief Force as a Trooper and from thence the British South Africa Police. In another case, by chance an indistinct photograph came to hand that showed a Fred Crewe at a mine in Northern Rhodesia in 1897 about 600 miles north of Bulawayo. With such an uncommon name in such a sparsely populated area, it is almost certain that this miner from the wilds of darkest Africa was the same Lieutenant Crewe of the Natal Mounted Rifles who in 1896 gallantly attempted the rescue of a trooper whose horse was killed under him and who was at the mercy of the enemy, during the fight at Umgusa, Matabeleland. This must also, sadly, have been the Captain F. Crewe who died in the Boer hospital after being wounded and captured with Captain McLaren, following Plumer's failed attempt to relieve Mafeking on 31st March 1900.

All the officers whether Regular British Army, Police or locally recruited and commissioned, with the exception of Lieutenant Murchison who was convicted of shooting Mr Parslow, a war correspondent (probably whilst drunk) seem to have provided the determination and leadership, both in action or under bombardment, expected of officers. Even Murchison seems to have behaved with valour when as we shall see, the Boers made their final assault in May 1900 and he and another military prisoner were temporarily released and issued with rifles to help with the defence of the town. Unlike the reported behaviour of other locally recruited units elsewhere in the War that have been reported to have been unsteady under fire, and prone to looting. The future Earl Haig described local mounted units, in a letter to his sister, as 'Scallywag cavalry'. Perhaps the greatest controversy of the siege has been the relationship between Captain Kenneth McLaren and Colonel Baden-Powell. Baden-Powell had requested McLaren join his expedition and McLaren had been ordered to South Africa to meet that request. McLaren's career since 1890 had been that of a high flyer. In 1890 he had been ADC to GOC Cavalry Brigade, Aldershot, Lord Wolseley, and moved with him when Lord Wolseley took up the post of GOC Ireland in 1891. From 1891 to 1895 McLaren was regimental adjutant and then from 1896-98 was ADC to GOC North Western District again moving with General Sir Baker Russell to Southern District from where he was ordered to South Africa and Baden-Powell's force. It is likely that Baden-Powell arranged for McLaren to join him to enable him to see some active service after nine years as ADC and adjutant, a necessary requirement for McLaren's future career.

Much has been made of the fact that Baden-Powell had to be "restrained" by his staff not to try to disguise himself to visit "The Boy" in the Boer hospital, although this would seem to be just exactly the exciting sort of lone adventure that would have appealed to Baden-Powell. Historians have tried to suggest that an improper relationship existed between the pair, most recently Pat Hopkins, a South African, has raised the matter again in the press[7]. Certainly Baden-Powell expended considerable time and energy in trying to get the wounded McLaren transferred from the Boer hospital where he was being treated after being wounded and captured.

Any anxiety Baden-Powell felt on hearing that McLaren had been wounded would have been compounded by the fact that he would certainly have felt responsible for a fellow regimental officer of the 13th Hussars, and being the Senior Officer, it would have been natural for him to make every effort on McLaren's behalf. On top of that McLaren was a friend and obviously a particularly well known and popular officer. McLaren also seems to have been an exceptionally well liked person outside the regiment. Major Baillie wrote, when the mistaken news of McLaren's death reached him: 'Regret and sympathy barely express my own feelings, and how many of us are there scattered about the world, who when they see the next polo tournament, will think again of the best of players, the nicest of fellows…'[8].

Secondly, Baden-Powell's knowledge of Boer hospitals would almost certainly have been coloured by Lady Sarah Wilson's reports of her experiences of such places, especially at Vryberg where she had visited some wounded British in the Boer Hospital in November before she was caught by the Boers and sent into Mafeking: 'Boer doctoring was of the roughest description, the surgeon's only assistant being a chemist-boy, and trained nurses were replaced by a few well meaning but clumsy Dutch girls, while chloroform or sedatives were quite unknown'[9]. It is no wonder the Commanding Officer of

Mafeking was upset to think of a friend being held and treated under those conditions. It is instructive also to read Baden-Powell's Staff Diary of the period. He expressed his concerns for all the wounded in the Boer Hospital and sent comforts to all under the white flag. Baden-Powell's diary, rather than dwelling on McLaren, is full of experiments for signalling by light to more directions than one by means of heliograph mirrors and a signal lantern and other routine matters.

Sadly the civil community in the town did not always display the same steadfastness of spirit as the military. Major Baillie notes that it was only after the expiry of the Kruger ultimatum that the local town council permitted serious preparations for the defence of the township. He says: 'The defences at this time consisted merely of a few breastworks, wagons drawn across the end of streets and a few strands of barbed wire fastened up on these points'. As we shall see, on more than one occasion Colonel Baden-Powell had to deal with defeatist rumours and "grousing" about the rations and the duties. Mr Whiteley, the Mayor, seems to have supported Baden-Powell and Mr Bell, Civil Commissioner and Resident Magistrate, was helpful in procuring the support of the African population. He is always reported as being cheerful. Messrs Whiteley and Bell were posted in orders at the start of the siege as being in charge of Reserves, though quite what these were is difficult to fathom as Colonel Hore is posted in the same Order as Commandant of Reserve Troops.

There was, as we shall see, some tension between the colonials particularly those of "Dutch" extraction and the Imperial Authorities. In one case a Mr de Kock was arrested for allegedly advising inhabitants not to hand over to the Commissariat certain groceries, as they were instructed to do. Although his case was dismissed it was indicative of the degree of resentment felt for the military authorities by certain sections of the populace. There was a feeling that some of the Cape Dutch inhabitants, a number of whom had relatives amongst the Boers, were corresponding with the enemy and there are pictures in contemporary magazines of bearded men being marched under escort to the gaol. These must have been the unwary ones; on October 9th Baden-Powell had issued a notice warning all spies to leave the town two days before the War started. Nurse Craufurd notes in her diary that one unnamed Irishman was arrested for High Treason in the early days of the siege; it seems that he was heard to say he was a Fenian and refused to take the oath of allegiance on joining the Railway Volunteers. Audrey Renew clearly identifies two Fenians arrested on a charge of High Treason as the 'Stationmaster, Quinlan, and Whelan (Hampson's clerk)'. At no time however, were military operations jeopardized by the activities of these dissenters in the town.

Despite the dissenters the majority of the men, loyal to the Crown, enrolled in one or other of the volunteer corps; Railway employees joining the Railway Volunteers—Mafeking owed its existence to the Railway, which was, no doubt, the largest employer—whilst others joined the Town Guard. This Town Guard had a very cosmopolitan membership; according to figures provided by Major Goold-Adams it comprised:

| | |
|---|---|
| British | 378 |
| Germans | 4 |
| Americans | 4 |
| Russians | 6 |
| Dutch | 27 |
| Norwegians | 5 |
| Swedes | 2 |
| Arabs and Indians | 15 |
| Total | 441 |

However, Colonel Stirling in his book, *The Colonials in South Africa*, which describes the various volunteer regiments and corps and their participation in the Boer War, gives a figure of 296 for the Mafeking Town Guard, so it may be that Goold-Adams's figures include the Railway Volunteers. The

Town Guard members were not always well behaved; on the day Kruger's ultimatum expired, the very day that war broke out, J.E. Westland is posted in Orders as being struck off strength from the Town Guard for gross misconduct. The Town Guard were very much the older men of the town; some were old soldiers; one at least had served in the Crimean War of 1854. Others were not fully fit, one having a wooden leg. They were employed as a reserve of last resort and were not, so far as can be ascertained, used to man any of the outer forts or redoubts. They were employed within the township area, and it was not until 10<sup>th</sup> February, when Councillor Dall, sub-Commandant of C Section of the Guard, was killed by a shell from "Creeky"[10] which cut him in half, that the Town Guard suffered any casualties. Even then it is not clear whether Mr Dall was killed whilst on military duty or whilst in the course of his employment.

The Railway Volunteers under command of Lieutenant J.R. More on the other hand did build and man a redoubt. On the eve of war breaking out, on 11<sup>th</sup> October, Nurse Crawfurd notes in her diary: 'Jim [her brother-in-law] and Mr Walmisley brought the Railway men up to the redoubt at the top of the Railway Camp and drilled them... It was so funny to see the men in their engine driver and other work clothes, and they were all laughing and joking to each other. They each had just a belt of cartridges and a rifle.' James (Jim) Buchan was appointed to the rank of honorary Lieutenant during the siege. Oddly, it seems that apart from providing a crew to drive the armoured train, the Railway men were not the ones to man it; that seems to have been the province of one or other of the Police forces, often under Lieutenant A.D. Murray.

Others who featured in the siege in a military capacity were Captain Goodyear in charge of the Colonial Contingent, otherwise known as the Cape Boys. Mr Webster ran the Native Contingent—these seem to have been the Baralongs who were prepared to defend the stadt. Mr McKenzie with the "Black Watch", formed from Africans who were refugees in the town.

Finally, mention must be made of the Cadet Corps, from which the Boy Scout Movement likes to trace its origin. The Cadets were set up to occupy the time and energies of some of the boys in the town too young to bear arms. It is in dispute as to whether it was Baden-Powell himself or Lord Edward Cecil who first conceived the idea of employing these youths to run messages about the town. They were certainly under the command of Lord Edward Cecil, in his capacity as Chief Staff Officer in the town, but it was Baden-Powell who recognized the keen response of the boys when provided with a structured and disciplined organization. It was he who had the vision to recognize that what boys could do under the difficult siege conditions of Mafeking could be adapted and extrapolated to all boys under all conditions, wherever they were. Baden-Powell also had the stature and international reputation after Mafeking, as well as his already well developed interest in training, to harness and direct youthful enthusiasm, developing it into the world wide Scouting movement, once he had retired from the Army.

The Cadets were set up on Saturday 10th February 1900 and were established as a Corps in a Daily Order on the 24th March. Lord Edward Cecil was appointed Commandant with Lieutenant Ronnie Moncrieffe as Lieutenant. The Establishment for the corps was: one Sergeant Major at 2/6d (12½p) per day, one Sergeant at 2/4d (11½p) per day, two Corporals at 2/3d per day and 14 privates at 2/- (10p) per day. Initially they used donkeys to take messages out to the more remote forts and redoubts of the defences. However, as the food situation worsened and more and more animals found their way into the soup pot, they were gradually issued with bicycles on which to perform their duties.

---

1    Nicknames were obviously as common in the Mess then as they are today. There was a Lieut "Ding" McDougall and Captain "Pa" Braithwaite to mention two, Baden-Powell was known as "Bloater"—See Hillcourt p. 56.

Nicknames, of course, are a symptom of the strong bonding amongst the regiment's officers that helped to build the regimental spirit.

2   At this time it was not uncommon for officers to write pamphlets on their own initiative unlike today when such books have to receive official blessing. Indeed officers often acted as correspondents for newspapers when on active service. Baden-Powell more than once earned money through his articles submitted to papers and was approached by *The Graphic* to act as correspondent in Sudan at one point whilst a serving officer. Today any officer writing for publication must submit his text for scrutiny and clearance by the Public Information Dept of the MOD.

3   Both Douglas Haig and R.S. Godley, brother of Sir Alexander Godley and author of *Khaki and Blue*, use the term.

4   See Major Haig's (later Earl Haig) letter to his sister quoted in Philip Warner's *Field Marshal Earl Haig*, p. 75.

5   FitzClarence was one of the first officers to transfer to the Irish Guards on their formation after the Boer War.

6   The Northern Rhodesia Journal No V, 1954, p. 62.

7   *Daily Mail*, 12 February 1999.

8   Major F.D. Baillie, *Mafeking: A Diary of the Siege*, p.190 (short title Baillie Siege).

9   Lady Sarah Wilson, *South African Memories*.

10  This was the name, sometimes spelt "Creechy" or "Grietjie" by which the Boer 94 pounder Creusot siege gun was usually known in the town. Other names were "Big Ben" or "Au Sanna" by the Africans.

## Chapter 3

## Role of the European ladies and non-European communities

It comes as something of a surprise to a modern researcher that Victorian officers ordered to a war zone took their wives with them. Of course, at this time, officers were responsible for the expense of their families; disturbance allowances were things of the distant future. If an officer could afford it there was no objection to his taking his wife along and the wife often provided her own contribution to the campaign.

The wives of three of the British officers who were at Mafeking travelled out with their husbands: Lady Violet Cecil, Lady Charles Cavendish-Bentinck and Mrs Godley, later Lady Godley. A fourth, Lady Sarah Wilson, wife of Captain Gordon Wilson, was already out in Africa. Lady Cecil (as described in the preceding chapter) started on the journey north, travelled as far as Kimberley with her husband but, after an unpleasant experience, decided to return to Cape Town. There she joined forces with Lady Cavendish-Bentinck in becoming a leading society hostess and the confidante of Sir Alfred Milner. Lady Cecil was, also, reputedly a great favourite with General Buller when he arrived in Cape Town to command the expeditionary force, so much so that Buller took her into his confidence when he sneaked away to Natal, against the wishes of the Cape administration, to take command of his Army's operations on the ground. Buller left her to break the news of his departure, after he had left, to Sir Alfred Milner. She certainly made a lasting impression on the High Commissioner, as on the death of her husband in 1921, she married him to become Viscountess Milner.

Mrs Godley accompanied her husband to South Africa and travelled with him up country, staying with a series of friends in Rhodesia. During the period of the siege, Mrs Godley was staying in Bulawayo and her husband reports in his book that he maintained a regular correspondence with his wife throughout. Letters were written on tissue paper and concealed in the lining of hats or soles of shoes by the African runners and he always sent a duplicate by the next runner. After the siege he checked with his wife and found that she had received all but one of his letters, either the original or the duplicate, and that he had received most of hers written to him[1].

Lady Sarah Wilson[2] was much more adventurous. She was an extraordinary person in that she demonstrated the courage, drive and determination that so characterizes the Churchills and which was so evident in the life of her nephew Winston. Her book, recounting her experiences at Mafeking and her other trips to Southern Africa, shows her to have been an extremely forceful person, not afraid to "rough it". Her style is purely narrative and rarely provides the sort of insights one can gain from a diarist; she never really drops her guard. This reticence may well derive from an aristocratic dislike of exposing herself and her family to public scrutiny; for instance her book scarcely mentions her husband and the only letter to him quoted, concerns her arrival in the Boer camp. It is formal and shows no endearment thus providing no indication of their relationship.

Lady Sarah had accompanied her husband, Captain Gordon Wilson of the Blues on a shooting trip to Rhodesia (in those days it was possible for officers to obtain a long leave of absence from the regiment for such sorties). During August or September

1899, whilst Baden-Powell was organizing the setting up of his two regiments of irregulars he met Gordon Wilson in Bulawayo and arranged for him to join his organization as his Aide de Camp. Thus the Wilsons, husband and wife, were in Mafeking in early October.

When war was imminent, on the advice of Baden-Powell, Lady Sarah moved out of town with her maid to stay with the Frasers. They ran the hotel and store at Setloguli, 35 miles south of Mafeking in Bechuanaland, on the road from Kimberley, from whence eventual help was expected to arrive. But with the Boer attack on the armoured train at Kraaipan only a few miles away, Lady Sarah decided to move further away from Mafeking to Mosita where she stayed with the Keeleys. There, she set up a "native courier service" into Mafeking sending in such news as she could obtain.

Lady Sarah stayed undiscovered in Mosita for some weeks until she attempted to contact her husband and Baden-Powell, in Mafeking, using a carrier pigeon provided by Mr Pearson, a Reuters' correspondent. He had escaped from Mafeking and was passing through Mosita on his way to Cape Town. The pigeon, it seems flew to Mafeking, but instead of returning directly to its loft at Mr Wirsing's home, landed on the roof of the Boer headquarters, where it was shot, and her message intercepted. Thus she was discovered by the Boers and placed under house arrest while they tried to decide what to do with her. In the end she took her fate into her own hands by driving to the Boer encampment outside Mafeking, demanding to see General Snyman, the Boer general in charge of the siege, and requesting a safe conduct to allow her to enter Mafeking and join her husband.

She was held a prisoner in the Boer hospital outside Mafeking for several days until she was eventually exchanged in early December for a horse thief in Mafeking gaol named Viljoen. She was reportedly accorded '...every consideration due to her sex by the Boers despite the fact that they might have made her position somewhat unpleasant since she had quite voluntarily taken up active participation in the siege by endeavouring to keep the garrison supplied with news'. Lady Sarah, on her arrival in Mafeking, became the leading lady in the social hierarchy; she had a special dugout built for herself as soon as she arrived, which was the talk of the town. Her dugout was 15 feet square and eight feet high. One wall was decorated with the Union Jack and she had space for her bed and a table, at which she and her husband were able to entertain Baden-Powell and five of his staff to Christmas dinner. The picture of the inside of the "bomb-proof" shows only a single bed so presumably her husband was expected to sleep elsewhere, although she did nurse him in her dugout, for a week during January, when he had an attack of peritonitis.

On the threat of war, in Bulawayo, while Baden-Powell and Gordon, her husband, travelled back and forth attempting to raise the two regiments, she 'took a course of ambulance lessons, learning how to bandage by experiment on the lanky arms and legs of a little black boy'. This experience of first aid together with her formidable organizing ability came in extremely useful when she was asked by Colonel Baden-Powell to set up and manage, with Miss Craufurd, a private nurse in Mafeking, a convalescent home in the Railway Institute after the disastrous attack on Game Tree. This convalescent home was set up as the number of casualties from the attack overwhelmed the facilities of the Victoria Hospital and it was essential to vacate beds by moving patients, who were on the way to recovery, to another location. A number of other ladies were called upon to assist with the nursing: Mrs Hayes, Dr Hayes's wife, Mrs More, Mrs Gemmel and Mrs Werner.

Lady Sarah and the ladies had no sooner sorted out the place, with beds set up and made, than the hospital wagons arrived with their 16 patients. At that very moment, ' "Creechy" sent off one of her projectiles which burst...about 100 yards beyond the improvised hospital having absolutely whizzed over the approaching ambulance vehicles'. Happily, no one was injured, and Lady Sarah went each day to the improvised hospital to oversee its administration. She writes that the proximity to the Railway Workshops, which the Boers knew were being used for the manufacture of shells by the garrison, meant that they persistently fired shells in that direction and this made the walk to and from the place 'exciting'. After three weeks the building was hit and the roof destroyed but happily the explosion injured none of the patients. However, they had to be evacuated to the Convent which, despite shell damage, had to be brought into use as a temporary hospital. As she herself was suffering from severe tonsillitis at the time, the doctor decided that both she and her husband, recovering from his peritonitis, should also go to the Convent. The nuns by this time had abandoned the place and were living underground in a bombproof shelter.

In addition to her work with the convalescent home, Lady Sarah Wilson contributed to the general morale of the besieged by her presence. She provided a children's party at Christmas and took a lead in charitable events in the town. She was often called on as "first lady" of the town to present prizes after the Sunday competitions. There is little doubt that her strength and determination in bearing the deprivations and discomforts of the siege provided an inspiration to all the others, men and women, in the town.

But what of the women who had homes in Mafeking? When the likelihood of a siege became inevitable and on the eve of the outbreak of war, in the middle of the morning of Wednesday 11th October, whilst Kruger's ultimatum was "ticking away", Baden-Powell sent a trainload of women and children south to Cape Town. It was an attempt not only to get them out of the war zone but also to reduce the mouths to feed. It was a 'fearfully sad sight, many women sobbing and clinging to their husbands'. The train was apparently so crammed that some who wanted to go could not find seats and were left behind. Another "special" was tried again next day but by then the ultimatum had expired and war had broken out. The Boers broke the line and the train had to return after a few miles. Thus, there were 229 white women and 405 white children shut up in Mafeking by the siege. Some of these were of Dutch origin who had family ties with the Boers and who favoured the enemy. However irrespective of origin, once the Boers started their bombardment of the town, Colonel Baden-Powell had a settlement constructed at Rowland's farm, on the edge of the defended area, for all women and children except the Africans who continued to live in the stadt, the African township. It is possible that Colonel Baden-Powell believed at the time that the African population would not become involved in the war. The women and children had to spend the week in the camp, unless they were given special dispensation, only coming into town on Sundays. The ladies[3] who were permitted to live in town were those who had undertaken ambulance training, as First Aid was called. Courses had been run in the weeks leading up to the war for the ladies to enable them to offer some practical skills in the event of a conflict.

Baden-Powell, himself, described the safety precautions that were taken for their security against being shelled. 'For the safety of the women and children a large underground gallery was made which accommodated the whole 600 of them and from which trenches were run out in order to provide play grounds and washing places in the open air but protected from projectiles'. Being in a special women's camp did not save the women from shelling and there were numerous incidents reported of the women's laager being targeted by the Boer guns; and there were casualties. Although the African women were not included in the women's laager and continued to live in the stadt, the Cape Coloured women were. One of this group of women, Mrs Graham, was an early casualty; she was injured on 4th November in the women's laager and whilst she was in hospital a fragment of a shell which burst nearby, entered the ward in the hospital where she was and she reportedly died of fright. There were ugly rumours too in the women's laager, that the Dutch women seemed to know in advance when the laager was to be shelled and took cover in good time, though whether the Dutch women really were in communication with the enemy was never discovered.

As perhaps should be anticipated in an age when women were not expected to participate in warfare, the names and deeds of individual women do not feature widely in the journals of the times. However, Mrs Ada Cock's letters to her sister Emily Fuller have survived. Ada's husband worked for his brother-in-law Harry Fuller, as manager of his cattle ranch a few miles outside Mafeking. On the threat of hostilities Willie Cock moved his family, comprising Ada and their four children together with all his stock, into Mafeking. Throughout the siege Ada maintained a one way correspondence with her sister who lived elsewhere in Cape Colony describing her life and the day-to-day domestic problems she was faced with in the besieged town. She had many narrow escapes from the shells, and it was the constant shelling which really got her down. Her husband was initially taken into the Town Guard and then into the Bechuanaland Rifles Volunteers. He spent a considerable amount of time on duty in the trenches around the town or later in the outer defence line. He was rarely at home at night and Ada had to cope with the children and siege life as best she could on her own. These are not letters full of bravado but rather a record of day-to-day domesticity: coping with food shortages especially in the later months, children's illnesses and a relating of rumours that circulated—what the Boers were up to and the progress of the relief column (mostly wishful thinking).

Of others who lived in the town we read that Mrs McCallum was very popular with the patients in the hospital, but not why. At the Grand Exhibition held on Sunday 25th March, Miss Campbell came away with the prize for fancy work, Mrs Ada Cock took the prize for a siege waltz[4] and Mrs Gates for a dressed doll. There was one wedding during the period of the siege, in April, when an unnamed Dutch girl, who spoke no English, married a private of the Bechuanaland Rifles who spoke no Afrikaans. Baillie's comment at the time was 'Let us hope it is a good omen of the future settlement of South Africa with the British as "Boss"'. Ada Cock records at least three babies born to white women during the siege. Brian Gardner's book has a picture of the time entitled *A British Amazon—Mrs Davies in the trenches* showing a female figure in a floral dress aiming a rifle over the parapet of a trench, but there is no written record of such an incident in the authorities consulted by this study.

There were those ladies who contributed directly to the defences and who were permitted to live outside the women's laager. These were mainly those helping to man the hospitals of which there were four in addition to the town's Victoria Hospital. Whether all these were manned throughout the siege is unclear but it seems that initially the fear of the consequences of the Boer bombardment prompted the authorities to make extensive provision for casualties. Some of these auxiliary hospitals were not large and probably were little more than dressing stations. For instance Nurse Craufurd records that on the afternoon of the 12th October: 'Mrs Lake and I went to see the room fitted up for the hospital she is to work at, and see that everything was ready'. At the Victoria Hospital, Matron Hill was in charge with Staff Nurse, Mrs Parminter, and two nurses assisted by the nuns from the Convent under Sister Joseph. Nurse Craufurd was a private nurse, more a medical companion, as she seems not to have been a trained hospital nurse. Her sister, Helen Buchan, was married to Jim Buchan, an employee of the Railway and, during the siege, the third in charge of the Railway Volunteers.

After three days of working with Lady Sarah Wilson at the Railway Institute Convalescent Home in late December Nurse Craufurd was asked by Baden-Powell to set up a small hospital for women and children. 'There have been several more deaths at the women's laager, and there is a lot of fever there, so I have been asked by the Colonel to take charge of a small hospital for women and children, as there is no room at the Victoria Hospital'. Her 'hospital' was a cottage, 'some way from town, but not very far from the women's laager and quite near the BSA Police Barracks... It is really the sergeants' mess room'.

The little hospital was very busy during January and February. Nurse Craufurd writes that it was full from the moment it opened and she could have done with more beds. Her cases were mostly children with some women, a few from the town but mainly from the women's camp. There were some cases of typhoid, several of malaria, dysentery, pneumonia, tonsillitis and one case of diphtheria. Although the doctor, Dr Tom Hayes, wanted her to have another nurse to assist her, Miss Craufurd preferred to have just her maid and a native servant. Miss Cowan who lived nearby came in for an hour each morning and, 'is kind enough to take night duty for me when I have a bad case'.

The site of this "hospital", near the BSAP barracks, provided Nurse Craufurd with an exciting and memorable day during the final Boer attack led by Commander Eloff on 12th May. She was woken in her sleeping quarters, a short distance from the hospital itself, at 5.45 am by the sound of firing close by, and her maid shouting out that the stadt was on fire. She got up quickly and with her maid, Elsie, ran, under fire, to the hospital building, 'Shall I *ever* forget that run? Bullets seemed to come from all around, whizzing near us, and our legs seemed as if they would not move fast enough. Elsie fell, and I thought she was hit; but I helped her up and she ran on. We stopped and crouched by the mortuary, a small iron shanty, and rushed on again'.

As they ran to the hospital they spotted a crowd of people running from the stadt towards the BSAP Fort and thought that they were natives rushing to the Fort for protection. On arrival at her hospital, once she had regained her breath, she went in to see if her patients were safe. All this time the building was being hit by rifle fire. After a little there was cheering heard from the Fort and those in the hospital wondered what it signified. Then shortly afterwards they became aware that there were Boers in the Fort so Elsie left for the women's laager and the native boy ran off to the Stadt leaving Nurse Craufurd and her sister Helen who had been on night duty, with the patients. Eventually the Boers finding the hospital so conveniently close to the BSAP Fort commandeered it and sent over their wounded with a German "ambulanceman". One of the wounded needed his arm amputated but the Boers had no doctor with them. It was agreed that Helen should go for Dr Tom Hayes, whose responsibility the hospital was, accompanied by a Boer, to see if the doctor would come. This also provided Helen with an opportunity to go to the railway camp where her baby was being looked after at Mrs Moore's house, to check his safety. The trip had to be undertaken under fire and the Boer was very unhappy, but both made the trip safely. Dr Hayes, the PMO and brother of Dr Tom, together with a medical student, Mr Young, Helen and the Boer returned under a Red Cross Flag to the laager hospital.

While Helen had gone in search of the doctor, Nurse Craufurd busied herself tearing up linen to make dressings. As it was a fever hospital, she did not have facilities and equipment for the treatment of wounds. She disarmingly states, 'I had had no experience in dressing wounds'. While engaged in tearing up sheets she was surprised to be approached by a Boer with a white flag bringing her a message: 'Hope you are all right; the Colonel [Colonel Hore], Williams, Smith and self with 18 others are prisoners'.

On reading this note she requested to see the prisoners and was taken back by the Boer with the white flag and was allowed to visit the prisoners in the small outhouse where they were being held. Captain Singleton, who was presumably the one who had sent the note, was apparently slightly wounded and his man had been killed. The others, Miss Craufurd reports, as being very downcast and anxious to know what had occurred in the town. She was unable to give them much comfort as all she knew had been what the Boers had told her, and it was not until her sister returned that the true position became clear. Why had Singleton sent that note? Was there some romantic attachment between Nurse Craufurd and Captain Singleton? If she were needed in a medical capacity surely Colonel Hore himself would have sent for her? Why did she rush to make the hazardous trip from her safe hospital to visit the prisoners? Unfortunately her diary offers no further clue.

After visiting the prisoners she returned with the same Boer to her hospital. Her record provides an insight into Boer morale at the time. He apparently told her, as they were dodging bullets, that he and, 'lots of others were only anxious that the war should end, and they hardly cared how, so long as they could go back to their farms in peace'. By this time Helen and the doctor had returned and the amputation of the young Boer's arm was carried out on the kitchen table. The doctor then saw to the other patients and finally went across to the Fort to see to one of the Cape Police troopers who had been badly wounded.

One woman who showed particular bravery that day was Annie Phaal a former old servant to Nurse Craufurd. Seeing Elsie in the laager and hearing that she had abandoned the hospital, she set out under fire to walk to the hospital to be with Miss Craufurd and to offer her assistance. She stayed to help for the rest of the day. There was some trouble with feeding all the patients as no rations had been issued, but a convalescent patient helped with the cooking. The only food available to the staff and the patients was sago boiled in water. During the day a Veldt-Kornet Eckstein died in the hospital. Later in the day Nurse Craufurd and Annie were able to take tea across to Colonel Hore and the British prisoners.

At about 6 pm, Major Hanbury-Tracy came to the hospital, under a white flag, with orders from Baden-Powell to evacuate it and take all the patients to the Victoria Hospital. It was dark by the time the ambulance wagon was loaded and ready to move. A man rode ahead with a white flag followed by the wagon and then Nurse Craufurd, her sister, Helen, Major Hanbury-Tracy, the doctor, and the walking Boer wounded followed up by a native servant with a large pile of blankets carried on his head. Owing to the darkness the procession came under friendly fire from the Railway Volunteers but happily no one was hurt and after a brief halt to confer with the Boers in the Fort they all proceeded to the main Hospital.

In Major Baillie's account of that final Boer attack and the surrounding of Eloff's men in the BSAP fort, he says: 'Mrs Buchan and Miss Crawford (sic) worked most calmly and bravely under fire. All the other ladies did their duty too. ...Mrs Winter was running about getting us coffee'.

All the women of Mafeking, both those who were in a position to contribute to the defence as well as those who were not, displayed steadfastness in the face of deprivation, shortage of food and physical danger. Doubtless their determination to overcome the dangers and hardship provided inspiration to their menfolk in the volunteer corps who were manning the perimeter defences, strengthening their resolve to win through.

**Non-white communities in Mafeking**
The predominant non-white or non-European group residing in the vicinity of Mafeking was the Baralong polity. After a protracted exodus from the north in the aftermath of the early 19th century *Mfecane*, the Baralong clans settled mainly on or around the Molopo River. At the time of the Siege, they numbered approximately 7,000 and their main economic activity centred upon cattle and sheep raising, and the maize mealie and vegetable production. The latter activity took place in and around the Stadt or African township area of Mafeking, consisting of between 100 and 200 huts. Their presence was to be of enormous military and economic benefit to both besieged and besiegers particularly in the context of cattle raiding and scouting for which they had acquired consummate and unrivalled skills particularly tracking over large distances. These particular skills were to be widely exploited by both Boer and Briton. Thus Cronje's and Snyman's forces secured the active and loyal support of the already closely-allied Rapulana-Baralong faction who provided numerous scouts, messengers, labourers and armed cattle guards, while the rival Tshidi-Baralong furnished similar services to Baden-Powell. Both factions were to exploit this dependency not only to facilitate the settling of old scores between them but also to extract rewards in cash and kind.

By the start of the siege these established Baralong communities led by Chief Wessels had been joined by up to 2,000 other African ethnic groups from as far away as Northern Rhodesia and Mozambique (principally Zambesians and Shangaanis) many of whom were skilled mine-workers driven

## Role of the ladies and non-European communities

out of the Transvaal mining centres by hostile Boer actions. Of these the Shangaanis were to prove the most vulnerable group during the coming severe rigours of the Siege.

Other ethnic groups included several hundred Fingos (traditional British allies) with their own small settlement area and the hundred or so "Cape Coloured" servants and labourers who were to provide crucial armed support to the garrison. Finally there were several score Asian traders who played a significant role in the food supply side of garrison life.

---

1  Sir Alexander Godley, *Life of an Irish Soldier*.
2  Lady Sarah Wilson was the sister of Lord Randolph Churchill and the aunt by marriage of FitszClarence who was married to Violet Spencer Churchill.
3  These were the wives of the prominent citizens and thus "ladies" rather than "women". A 19th century social distinction.
4  No record of this music has survived apparently—Midgley, *Petticoat in Mafeking*.

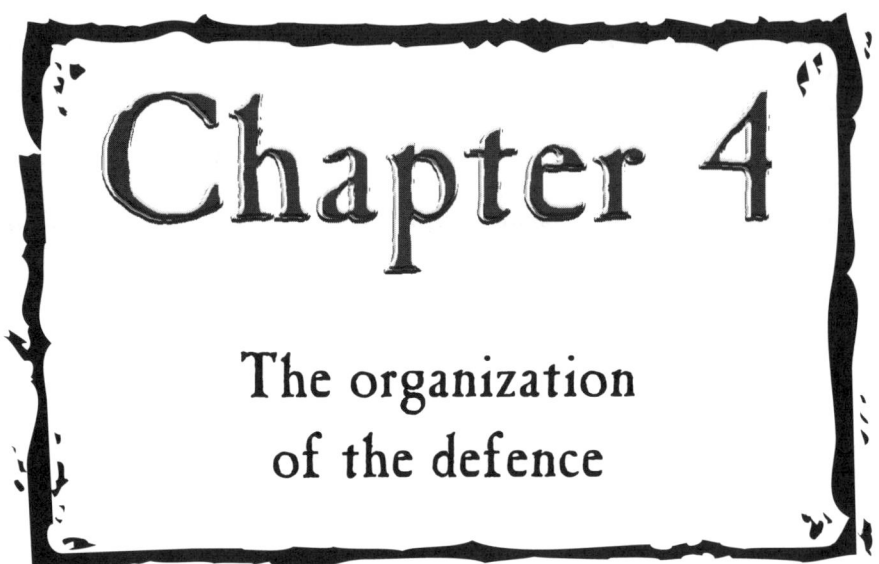

# Chapter 4

## The organization of the defence

Before embarking on a description of the siege, it is important to understand how the defence was organized. Colonel Baden-Powell set up his Headquarters in Dixon's Hotel, on the roof of which was built a lookout from which he could view almost all parts of the perimeter. Initial defensive measures, apart from setting up Baden-Powell's headquarters in Dixon's Hotel, included defining sectors on the perimeter and allocating commanders and troops to the sectors, running telephone lines from Dixon's Hotel to the dugouts where the various sector commanders had their headquarters to provide communication, and the laying of real and dummy dynamite mines around the approaches to the town. The laying of these mines which were fired electrically, was done under the observation of the Boers. Certainly it is inconceivable that intelligence about these preparations was not passed to the Boers in view of the ethnic and family connections some of the citizens of the town had with the enemy.

Major Baillie, who seems to have been a retired military officer acting as a correspondent for *The Morning Post*, has provided a quite detailed description of the defences of the town.

# The organization of the defence

The description following relies to a large extent on Baillie's although some additional details have come to light from other eyewitnesses, particularly Sol Plaatje. The map is based on that drawn by an officer present at the siege, again with some additional material gleaned from other authors.

## A description of the defences

Mafeking is situated on a rise about 300 yards north of the Molopo River, which flows roughly from east to west. At the turn of the century it was about three-quarters of a mile square. The railway ran to the west of the town, and practically speaking, due north and south, but immediately south where it crossed the Molopo by an iron bridge, it inclined rather westward for a distance of two or three miles. The railway embankment north and south of the river thus furnished cover from the east and south-east heights on the southern bank of the Molopo. To the west again of the railway, and nearly butting it half a mile south of the Molopo, was the native township or stadt, lying on both sides of the river, and on the northern bank, commencing about half a mile from the railway, then running in a north-westerly direction for about a mile and a half, and ending about a mile and three-quarters west of the railway. The ground in front of the northern end was slightly higher than the stadt and soon commenced to sink away from it, affording good cover to an enemy moving on that side. Near the railway the ground sloped gradually down for a considerable distance to the river. The country round Mafeking to the west, north and east, was flat, but across the Molopo to the south and south-east it commanded the town. The ground to the west of the stadt commanded the stadt.

Situated 2,000 yards south, and slightly east of the centre of the town, was an old fort of Sir Charles Warrens'—Cannon Kopje. This was the key to the position. It was an old circular stone fort with an interior diameter of approximately 25 yards, and only by an extraordinary amount of work, and that after it had been attacked by the Boers on 31st October, was it brought up to a state to enable it to resist even old ordinary seven-pounder guns. The "coloured township" occupied by the Cape Coloured population lay directly between Cannon Kopje and the town on the southern bank of the river. Following the course of the river eastward about 1,200 yards from the town, on the northern bank extended the Brickfields (eventually occupied by both parties), while in the same direction, and about three and a half miles from Mafeking, on a ridge, was MacMullen's farm that subsequently became the Boer headquarters. Returning to the town—at the north-eastern corner was the Convent. Due east of that, about a mile away, was the grandstand while north-north-east from the Convent, and a mile and a half away, was the base of the waterworks.

Thus we have the railway station at the north-west corner, the Convent at the north-east corner, Ellis's house at the south-east corner, and at the south-west corner, the pound; while in a line from the south-west corner of the town and the northern portion of the stadt, the BSAP barracks and fort (another Warren construction from the days of his Bechuanaland expedition) lay about mid-way. With the exception of a strip of scrub about a mile wide to the north and east of the Convent the country all round was almost bare.

The town was composed of one-storey houses built of soft bricks and roofed with corrugated iron, the only exception being the Convent of two storeys and the station, which was not yet complete. The stadt consisted of African huts and gardens. The BSAP fort was a duplicate of Cannon Kopje.

Baillie's estimate of Mafeking's peacetime population prior to the siege was 2,000 whites, 4,000 to 5,000 Africans in the stadt and about 500 inhabitants in the Coloured township. At the beginning of the siege he estimated there were approximately 1,500 whites, 7,000 natives in the stadt owing to native refugees, while the Coloured population remained unchanged at about 500.

The forces at Colonel Baden-Powell's disposal for the defence of this area were about 750 enlisted troops of various kinds—the Protectorate Regiment, the British South Africa Police, the Cape

## The organization of the defence

Police and the Bechuanaland Rifles. In addition there was a locally recruited Town Guard of 441[2], being all the able bodied, and one or two not so able bodied, men of the town, who had responded to "the call to arms" by the Mayor, Mr Whiteley, when it became clear that a siege would be set by the Boers. About 60 Cape Coloureds signed on for The Colonial Contingent more commonly known as the "Cape Boys" while the "Black Watch" were a number (reportedly about 300) of native recruits who it seems were not primarily from the local Baralong tribe, and who lived in the "Strangers' location" outside the township. These strangers, of whom Baden-Powell himself wrote: 'The native question has been a difficult one as the Boers sent in, on the outbreak of war, about 1,000 native refugees from Johannesburg—but they turned out to be a blessing in disguise—as being accustomed to mining work under white supervision, they were formed into groups and have done invaluable service on our defence works'. These African and Coloured recruits and the Town Guard were armed with obsolescent single shot Martini-Henry rifles and their own hunting rifles whilst the police and regimental troops had the relatively new Lee-Metford rifles with five shot magazines.

Colonel Baden-Powell therefore set about readying Mafeking for siege. He moved his forces into the town in September 1899 and ordered Lieutenant Colonel Vyvyan to take in hand measures for its defence. The available guns were 'two old seven pounders dated 1820 with very poor range but that made an impressive bang and lots of smoke; six good maxim guns that were to prove invaluable; a Nordenfeldt and a little screw mountain gun' as Major Godley was later to write. During the siege an old ship's cannon[3] was unearthed, christened "The Lord Nelson", and brought into action with home-made round shot. The Railway Workshops constructed a howitzer from boiler tubes, which was used in the latter days of the Siege.

In a siege where adaptation and making do was a way of life for the besieged, Lieutenant Daniels BSAP and late Glamorganshire Artillery Militia under Major Panzera BSAP, who commanded the artillery, designed and manufactured shells and fuses using unexploded Boer shells of which there seem to have been a good many. Bounties were offered for unexploded ordnance and there are several recorded deaths and injuries to people attempting to defuse shells and who were blown up. One of the cleverest and most significant adaptations was the fitting of enlarged driving bands to several hundred five pounder shells to enable them to be fired by the seven pounders. These five pounder shells had been left behind by Dr Jameson when he set out on his famous raid in 1895. The shells had apparently been buried for safety but were unearthed during the siege and, after modification, permitted the guns to continue firing when ammunition for the seven pounders was running low.

The perimeter of the defences was between five and six miles. Commencing with the Convent, and working westward at the outset, the defences were as follows: the railway line and armoured train protected the north-west front, then nearer to the railway came Fort Victoria, occupied by Railway Volunteers; and in the arc of a circle extending to the north end of the stadt, trenches occupied by the Protectorate Regiment at night. These were gradually turned into forts. The women's laager was established on the edge of the stadt, near the BSAP officers' quarters and a refugee camp in the hollow north of the stadt, the northern end of which was held by Captain Vernon and C squadron Protectorate Regiment, while B squadron, under Captain Marsh, and the natives, held the stadt itself—the whole under Major Godley, who commanded the western outposts. The town was garrisoned by the Cape Police under Captains Brown and Marsh. These and the Railway Volunteers were under Colonel Vyvyan, while Cannon Kopje was entrusted to Colonel Walford and the BSAP. Colonel Baden-Powell retained one squadron of the Protectorate Regiment as reserve under his own immediate control. These arrangements were subsequently much augmented.

After the Convent had been practically demolished by shell fire and the railway line all round the town pulled up or mined, a small work was erected at the Convent corner and garrisoned by the Cape Police and a Maxim under Lieutenant Murray. He was also put in charge of the armoured train, which had, however, been withdrawn to the railway station out of harm's way. The Railway Volunteers garrisoned the cemetery, and had an advanced trench about 800 yards to the front and immediately to the right of the railway line. To the westward came Fort Cardigan, and then Fort Miller. In the south-west was Major Godley's fort, at the north of the African stadt, with an advance fort—Fort Ayr—crowning the slope to the northern end of the stadt. Although this was rather detached, it commanded a view and fire for a great distance to the south of the northern portion of the stadt, and here the Cape Police were entrenched with the Maxim. At the south-western corner, and on the edge of the stadt Captain Marsh's fort was situated. Five hundred yards to the west front of Captain Marsh's[4] post lay Limestone Fort, commanding the valley, on the other side of which lay the Boer laager and entrenchments. The whole of the edge of the stadt was furnished with loopholes and trenches, and garrisoned by the African inhabitants. By the railway were situated two armoured trucks with a Nordenfeldt. Cannon Kopje, with two Maxims and a seven-pounder, lay to the south-east. 'The perimeter of the works at first was approximately seven miles; latterly it extended to a little over ten miles'[5].

And now to the immediate defence of the town. At the south-western corner was the pound, garrisoned by Cape Police, under Captain Marsh; then eastwards Early's Fort, Dixon's Redan, Dall's Fort, Ellis's Corner, with Maxim and Cape Police, under Captain Brown. On the eastern front, Ellitson's Kraal, Musson's Fort, De Kock's Fort, with Maxim, Recreation Ground Fort, and so back to the Convent, on the left of which lay the Hospital Fort—all these, unless otherwise mentioned, garrisoned by the Town Guard. These so-called forts were garrisoned with from 15 to 40 men, and furnished with head cover and bomb proofs against artillery. Bomb proofs were constructed everywhere largely on an individual household basis, although there is some evidence, according to Hamilton, that the local Baralong population were rather more fatalistic and tended not to provide themselves with secure shelters with solid overhead protection. There were traverses erected at the end of streets and trenches dug, giving cover leading from every portion of the town and defences; it was possible to walk round the town without being exposed to aimed fire. The trenches were constructed with a view to being manned in case of need. Telephones were established in all the headquarter bomb proofs of outlying forts, and connected with the headquarter bomb proof, thus securing instant communication and avoiding the chance of orderlies being sniped, which might otherwise have been the case. These defences were all improvised on the spot, every conceivable sort of material being utilized.

There seems to have been some controversy over the prolonged nature of the Siege at the time. Whilst the *Times* questioned the strategic value of the Mafeking Siege, Major Baillie repeated the arguments that led Lord Wolseley to send Baden-Powell to the area in the first place. There is no argument that the British presence in Mafeking diverted a considerable Boer force from sweeping down into Cape Colony. It is the longer-term maintenance of the defence that is questioned. Baillie argues that the loss of Mafeking would have created a loss of confidence amongst the African population of the area, and also would have provided the Boers with all the rolling stock in the Mafeking yards and the line from the Vaal River north. This would have opened Rhodesia to attack thus altering the 'whole condition of the war and not in our favour'. Besides it seems unlikely that a man as tenacious as Baden-Powell would have been prepared to hand over to the enemy what he had set out to defend just because of uncomfortable conditions being endured by non-combatants.

One might ask why the Boers themselves were so reluctant to carry out any attack in force. They had the artillery fire power to have laid down a heavy enough barrage to have destroyed British defensive positions opening the way for a major attack, but such an attack never materialized. Instead, the Boers seemed to believe that their random shelling would destroy the morale of the defence and it was not until the town was almost relieved that a serious attack was launched on 12th May 1900.

---

1   Sir Charles Warren's Bechuanaland expedition of 1884/5.
2   Figures supplied to Lady Sarah Wilson by Major Goold-Adams.
3   The authors, quite by chance, came across details of four other, similar ships' cannons in an articles in the *Northern Rhodesia Journal*. In one article *Artillery in Rhodesia, 1890-1896* by Roger Summers published in the *Northern Rhodesia Journal No VI*, is added *A Further Note on cannon* in which it says that: 'In the National Museum, Bulawayo are two of Lobengula's cannon, one of which is almost identical with the Lusaka cannon, mentioned and pictured in *Journal No.V*, and bears similar markings cast above the trunnions, i.e. the letters B P below a crown. Sir James Mann, Keeper of the Armouries at the Tower of London, very kindly identified the makers as Boulton and Paul of Norwich and gave the date of the piece as about 1800'.
    The similarity of the markings on these two guns plus the two in Northern Rhodesia with the markings on the "Lord Nelson" at Mafeking shows that they came from the same foundry and almost certainly came from the same British ship wrecked on the east coast.
4   This Captain Marsh, Protectorate Regiment should not be confused with Captain Marsh of the Cape Police.
5   Col J. Stirling *The Colonials in South Africa*, p.210. Sir Charles Warren's Bechuanaland expedition of 1884/5.
5   Figures supplied to Lady Sarah Wilson by Major Goold-Adams.

## Chapter 5

## The campaign

*No product here the barren hills afford,*
*but men of steel, the soldier and his sword*
    Goldsmith—*The Traveller*, 1764

Mafeking was a military operation in which only a minority of the participants were professional soldiers. On the British side there were the Imperial officers sent out with Colonel Baden-Powell. There were, of course, the officers and troopers of the Cape Police and the British South Africa Police, both paramilitary forces. The former were the police of the Cape Colony whilst the BSAP was a comparatively new force, set up in 1897 as a consequence of the Jameson Raid, to police Matabeleland and Mashonaland. Certain incidents had occurred in connection with police forces in Rhodesia and Bechuanaland before the Raid, creating the need for this new force. The Imperial authorities provided assurance that it would be commanded by officers seconded from the British Army in order to reassure President Kruger. It could be said, therefore, that the officers of the BSAP were also professional soldiers. The troopers of both forces were men experienced in living in southern Africa, used to spending days in the saddle and were accomplished shots.

Then, there were the volunteers, the Rhodesian Volunteers and the Bechuanaland Rifles Volunteers; these were militia style units based as their name suggests in Rhodesia and Bechuanaland. They undertook training on a regular basis and were held in readiness to support the authorities in times of emergency. Finally there were the irregular mounted infantry regiments raised in August 1899 by Colonel Baden-Powell, the Rhodesia Regiment commanded by Colonel Plumer and the Protectorate Regiment commanded by Colonel Hore. The men of the Rhodesia Regiment were on one-year contracts as the Regiment was disbanded on expiry of the year's service at the end of September 1900. The Protectorate Regiment seems to have had a longer life but, according to Stirling, they too were disbanded before the end of 1900.

For the Boers, their artillery was their only true professional force. The Free State artillery being established in 1880 by Major Albrecht[1], who remained in command until his capture at Paardeburg, while the Transvaal artillery was set up ten years later, in 1890[2]. Officers were sent overseas for training and soldiers signed up for three years. The suggestion, sometimes heard, that the Boer artillery was run by foreigners is incorrect, although a number of foreign volunteers did serve with the Boer guns. Commandants of commandos were, supposedly, selected for their military competence so they, too, could be considered professional soldiers.

The Boer forces had a very different organization from the British. All adult males of Afrikaner descent in the two Boer states, the Transvaal and the Orange Free State (OFS) had a duty to answer the call to defend the state in time of war; every man had an obligation to carry arms and to equip himself. The state also had the right, in times of war, to requisition private property for the prosecution of military operations. This almost feudal military system had evolved from the need for mutual protection in an alien land from the earliest times of the Dutch settlers in the Cape.

It had developed in later years from the need of the two young Boer States to protect themselves against aggressive native tribes. A Boer army was a levy of the Afrikaner citizens or burghers[3]. There was no requirement, as in European armies, for a Boer soldier to lose some of his rights and privileges as a citizen; no equivalent to the British "Army Discipline Act". There was no division between the political and military organization of the state; the burghers wore no uniform to distinguish between soldier or citizen. The men elected their officers; in practice this usually meant that civil leaders were also military officers.

The Boer army organization was based on electoral districts of which there were 22 in the Transvaal and 18 in the OFS. Burghers from an electoral district formed a commando. The commando was not a unit of specific size like a battalion; its size depended on its voters' roll, thus it could be as high as 3,000 in districts such as Pretoria or Pochefstroom or as low as 300 in less populated areas. The commanding officer of a commando was the Commandant, elected by the burghers and holding office for five years (three years in the OFS). As each electoral district was divided into electoral wards (wyks) so the burghers of each ward elected a Field Cornet (Veldt Kornet) as their commander for a period of office of three years. Whilst the Commandant was expected to be chosen as a military man, Field Cornets were elected as community leaders with responsibilities within their communities as Justices of the peace, registration officers, inspectors of "natives" and general government representatives. Military prowess was unlikely to feature high amongst the abilities for which they were elected. The Field Cornet kept the registration of those liable for military service and was responsible for seeing that they were properly mounted and equipped.

In the field the Field Cornet was assisted by several corporals, also elected by the burghers in the camp. He was responsible for the supply of ammunition, transport and supplies to his men. The commando usually had a Commissariat Officer from whom the Field Cornet drew his supplies; the actual distribution was down to the corporals.

## The campaign

The burghers were men who could shoot and ride but were not as amenable to discipline as trained troops nor was there any statutory means of enforcing it within this democratic, citizen army. This lack of discipline was apparent more than once amongst those besieging Mafeking. They joined their colours bringing their rifles and their own horses, in many cases as whole families—fathers, brothers, sons and uncles. It was probably this "intimate" organization, where the men of a commando were all known to one other, if not related, as much as the democratic nature of their force that made the Boers reluctant to accept the casualties they would have had to sustain if they had made a frontal attack on Mafeking.

Mafeking was a border town. In 1899, it was sited in the Cape Colony, close to the borders with the Transvaal and the Bechuanaland Protectorate. In 1895 it had been the town from which Dr Jameson launched his "raid" into the Transvaal. Apart from the notoriety derived from being the base for this incursion into a friendly state, Mafeking was mostly noted for being a railway town. It had, until six years previously, been the most northerly point to which the railway ran. Under pressure from Cecil Rhodes the railway was extended to Bulawayo, but Mafeking still remained an important railway town not only for its engineering workshops but also because it was the main access point for goods being sent to Bechuanaland.

As the opening months of the Boer War comprised so many setbacks for the British, the psychological effect of having at least one place where the Boers could be seen not to be getting "their way" and where a numerically greater Boer force was being withstood by the much smaller British one, was immense. Not just amongst the troops and colonials in South African but also at home in Britain, and this needs to be taken into account when considering the strategic importance of the town in the context of the whole war.

For the Boers, the town was firstly, of practical importance; the capture of Mafeking would have provided them with considerable railway assets in the form of locomotives and rolling stock together with railway access to Rhodesia. Secondly on a psychological level, its capture would be seen as retribution for being the staging post of the Jameson Raid.

Initially the Boers invested Mafeking with about 8,000 men. As has been described Colonel Baden-Powell established an approximately seven-mile perimeter which, during the course of the Siege, he expanded to a little over ten miles. The town was 1,000 yards square and its best feature from the point of view of the defender was that it was not commanded by hills. The trenches had good fields of fire; the ground outside being a flat plain for a considerable distance so that 'full advantage could be taken of the flat trajectory of the Lee-Metford rifles'[4]. It is astonishing that so small a British force could not only hold but also expand so large an area whilst opposed by such superior numbers. The tribute for this success has to go to Baden-Powell and his staff for their planning of the defences and the ruses used to discourage Boer attacks, such as the dummy minefields and the searchlights.

The British artillery throughout the Siege was commanded by Major Panzera of the BSAP and manned by men of that force. It comprised a number of obsolescent guns, augmented during the Siege by an old ship's cannon and a home-made 16-pounder howitzer. Powder, shells and fuses were manufactured in the railway workshop, often using unexploded Boer ordnance.

In opposition to this rather weak British garrison the Boers initially deployed 8,000 men under General Cronje equipped with modern artillery, one gun of which was a new Creusot 94 pounder Siege gun. During the period of the Siege this gun alone fired 1,497 shells into the town. Although Cronje departed after about six weeks, taking approximately half the force with him, General Snyman, who was left to continue the Siege, retained the Creusot and six other guns. Furthermore the Boers were equipped with modern Mauser rifles.

From the beginning of the Siege the Boers indulged in long range sniping at the town and barricades had to be erected at the end of streets to provide cover for people moving about in the town. Small limited actions took place almost daily at the forts and particularly in the Brickfields with the exchange of fire between opposing forts and trenches. There were, however, a number of larger scale actions the outcomes of which had an influence on the subsequent conduct of events.

**The Skirmish at Five Mile Bank**
The first of these took place on October 14th. A strong patrol from A Squadron, the Protectorate Regiment under Captain Lord Charles Cavendish-Bentinck, was probing north along the railway when, about four miles out of town, it came into contact with a strong force of Boers who were advancing down the line. The patrol fell back and called for support as the Boers who had two guns, pursued them and tried to cut them off. The armoured train with a Hotchkiss and a Maxim gun with 15 BSAP crew steamed out to support the retreating patrol. Meanwhile Colonel Baden-Powell ordered the 70 men of D Squadron the Protectorate Regiment, under Captain FitzClarence, to protect the right flank of the armoured train. The gunners in the armoured train put out of action one of the Boer guns and forced the other to withdraw from two other positions it tried to take up.

On its arrival D Squadron which was deployed in extended line, found the Boer line of about 400 men also extended and stretching well beyond their left flank. FitzClarence's squadron none the less attacked and the Boers began to fall back to a selected position, described by J. Angus Hamilton as 'admirably adapted to their method of fighting'[5]. This position was on a low ridge covered with 'timber, scrub, large masses of rock and cut up by many little sluits that extended along their line of retreat'. From this protected position the Boers were able to catch D Squadron on the open veldt with little or no cover.

This tactic of drawing the enemy onto a prepared selected position was a favourite one of the Boers and perhaps with more experience FitzClarence might have recognized the trap. D Squadron was caught in the open with little cover, and their situation became very serious. They held a front of about 80 yards while the Boers continued to extend their line trying to cut the squadron off from Mafeking and the armoured train, which by now was about three-quarters of a mile away. The inexperienced troopers of the Protectorate Regiment behaved with exemplarary courage and discipline, firing steadily at the enemy, apparently unaffected by the heavy odds against them. Just as their flank began to turn, Charles Cavendish-Bentinck with two troops and a seven-pounder gun arrived within range. After two shrapnel shells the Boers fell back and FitzClarence was able to extricate his men. On their arrival back in town they were cheered. Nurse Craufurd describes the scene: '...soon we heard cheering, and ran out and saw our troops coming home after the first fight. There were no women but us four—Mrs Reisle, Mrs Lake, Helen and I—but we waved to them and cheered them and they looked so tired, but smiled and waved their caps when they saw us. It was sad to see the riderless horses'[6].

The "riderless horses" were those of the casualties; astonishingly only two men had been killed, Troopers Walshe and Parland with two officers, Captain Lord Cavendish-Bentinck and Lieutenant Brady, and 13 Troopers wounded although one of the wounded would die later. Boer losses are given by Stirling as 53 killed including four Veldt Kornets and many wounded (J. Angus Hamilton quotes the figure of 107 wounded)[7].

One can only speculate on the reasons for this imbalance of casualties. Why should the Boers have lost so many when they are reported withdrawing to a prepared position with plenty of cover and the British were left coverless on lower ground? There are a number of possible explanations: perhaps the Boers, because they outnumbered the British by almost five to one, were over confident and careless. Perhaps the sheer recklessness of FitzClarence committing his 80 men against 400 may have so disconcerted the Boers that they became careless. Or, perhaps the British use of disciplined volley fire was more effective than the individual target selection and shooting of the Boers. One thing we do know, from Major Baillie, is that the use of khaki uniforms was in the British favour. Baillie writes:

*The campaign* 53

'Now to show the advantage of khaki as a fighting colour on the well-bleached veldt. (A galloper) rode up to the Boers and was fired upon. He then galloped along the front of, through and along the rear of our own men without seeing a man...In at least two occasions he was within 30 yards of his own men and could not see them. The dark clothing of the Boers is, however, more conspicuous, but with smokeless powder and khaki the firing line even at short ranges is invisible as a target'.

Here then is another reason for the greater number of Boer casualties and there can be no doubt that the result of this little engagement had a great and lasting psychological effect on the Boers.

**The first assault**
The Boers' first serious attempt to take the town began on 25th October with a heavy bombardment that commenced at 6.15 am. Later, during the day, at about noon, the heavy guns ceased and Boer troops were observed in considerable confusion, eventually sorting themselves out and advancing, on two sides of the town, in extended order under cover of the lighter guns and with a great expenditure of rifle ammunition. On the eastern side of the town they approached to within 2,000 yards and halted. Meanwhile on the western side of town the Boer advance was made on the native stadt. The defenders, two British squadrons, held their fire until the attackers were close and then opened fire with maxim and rifles They were supported by enfilading fire from the Baralongs with their shotguns and snyders, 'killing many' in the words of Major Baillie. Consequently the attack failed. Boer casualties are unknown but their ambulances were seen collecting bodies after the action. On the British side Nurse Craufurd observed, 'It seems marvellous that none of our men were killed. A native's eye was injured, and a man was brought into hospital having fallen from his horse from exhaustion'. This was not quite the true picture,

as Audrey Renew's chronology for the day indicates. Trooper Kelley, Protectorate Regiment, was wounded and subsequently succumbed.

All the observers of the action this day comment on the profligate use of rifle fire by the Boers from well beyond effective range. J. Angus Hamilton noted, '...Their expenditure of rifle ammunition and their extreme prodigality in shells was as much playing into our hands as reaping them any advantage', and Baillie felt that the rifle fire did more damage than the shells. The reluctance of the Boers to launch a determined frontal attack may well have been influenced by Kruger's instruction to Cronje to limit casualties to not more than 50 killed. The experience of the losses in the skirmish of the 14th October doubtless contributed to Cronje's lack of vigour in pressing this attack.

**Night attack on the Boer trenches**
Throughout this period the enemy had been encircling the town with breastworks and trenches, mostly at about 2,500 yards distance. The Boers took to lounging and relaxing on the parapets of their trenches, knowing themselves to be outside rifle and maxim range. Such behaviour was seen as a provocation by the defenders, and the Boers were not undisturbed in their "sun-bathing" as snipers and small groups were sent into "no man's land". Some trenches crept nearer to the town, to between 1,200 and 800 yards, particularly in the area of the Brickfields and these posed an especial nuisance and danger. Accordingly, Colonel Baden-Powell decided to take action against these closer enemy trenches, so on the night of the 27th October, he ordered an attack on the trenches commanded by Commandant Louw to the north of the Malmani road.

The attacking force comprised the same men of D Squadron, the Protectorate Regiment under Captain FitzClarence who had been involved in the skirmish on the 14th. They were supported by Lieutenant Murray and 25 men of the Cape Police. FitzClarence's men were ordered to use bayonets only. At about

9.00 pm, in the dark they silently penetrated the Boer lines to a point behind their objective without being discovered. Meanwhile the Cape Police who had been split into two parties, one considerably further east than the other, moved to the Brickfields in order to enfilade the rear of the Boer trenches. On his shout and brandishing his sword, Captain FitzClarence charged, jumping down into the Boer trench followed by his cheering men with their bayonets fixed. FitzClarence himself was credited with killing four of the enemy with his sword.

The Boers were taken completely by surprise, and commenced firing in all directions. To protect and cover the withdrawal of D Squadron after they had cleared the Boer trenches, the Cape Police opened fire on the rear Boer trenches and FitzClarence and his men were able to return to the town unmolested. In the darkness the Boers were in complete confusion and some of those fleeing to the rear from the British attack were fired on by their own troops. Boer losses have been stated to be as high as 100 killed and wounded whilst the British losses were six: Corporal Burt, Troopers Turner, Soundy, Middleditch, Fraser and McDonald killed; nine wounded, including Captain FitzClarence and Lieutenant Swinburne, and two captured. From the British point of view this had been a well-planned and executed operation with a very satisfactory outcome. The wounds sustained by FitzClarence and Swinburne were not serious and they were soon back on duty. The Boers claimed later that the trenches in question were manned only by young boys and that the British had massacred these youths who were sleeping there. Why the Boers had permitted young boys to sleep in the front line trenches of a war zone is not explained.

**Boer attack on Cannon Kopje**
There are few areas of relatively high ground around Mafeking. To the south of the township lies a hill about 200 feet high, with a jumble of rocks on the top, known as Cannon Kopje and it commands the town. On its summit was an old fort built at the time of the Warren Commission to Bechuanaland some 14 or 15

years previously. About a mile to the north-east on the same, southern bank of the Malopo there is another hill slightly higher than Cannon Kopje and occupied by a Boer fort. The African stadt nestles under the lee of the north-western slope of Cannon Kopje. If the Boers could capture the Kopje they could command the town. On 31st October they made their attempt.

From Jackal Tree about 3,400 yards SSW of Cannon Kopje the Boers pushed forward their artillery to about 2,000 yards from the Kopje. From this position and from their fort on the height to the north-east, at about 4.30 am, they opened fire on the fort on Cannon Kopje which was manned by Colonel Walford and 57 men of the BSAP with two maxims and a seven-pounder. After 30 minutes heavy shelling, during which no response could be made as the maxims and the men had to keep under cover, the Boer infantry attacked from the south-east coming to within 300 yards of the fort. The disciplined men in the fort set up their maxims and held their fire until the Boers were well within range when the maxims and volley firing from their rifles, together with the fire from a seven-pounder, 'run out under cover of houses near the south corner of town' and commanded by Lieutenant Murchison, stopped the Boer advance and drove them back. As Baillie described it: 'They (the Boers) attacked with great resolution, but our fire was held till they came within good range, and then after sustaining it for some time they broke and fled'. The British losses included Captain the Honourable D. Marsham and Captain Charles Pechell with six NCOs and men killed and three men wounded. Boer casualties are not reported although eyewitnesses again speak of ambulance wagons coming out to collect their dead and wounded. Baillie mentioned the fact that when the ambulances came onto the field under truce, a number of the Boers who were lying down and presumed to be casualties, got up and ran off. Hamilton estimated that the Boers probably lost in the region of 40 men.

J. Angus Hamilton had no doubt of the vital nature of the fort to the defence of the town and he expresses considerable criticism of the lack of preparation at the fort to meet an attack. He blamed Colonel Baden-Powell for 'the folly of leaving it unprotected... We have paid a heavy price for our neglect'. Overhead cover against shells and bullets was lacking and the men had to stand at the breastworks with their heads and upper bodies exposed when firing at the enemy because of insufficient preparation which had failed to provide them with loop holes. Hamilton also suggests that this successful action was of key importance in the Siege. The Boers had already assessed the importance of this position and, up to this point, had regularly shelled it. The attack, had it succeeded, would have almost certainly seen the fall of the town. Hamilton writes: 'The subjugation of this point (Cannon Kopje fort), in reality the turning point of the Siege, was, however, of vital concern to Commandant Cronje'. Cronje had men massed and ready, once Cannon Kopje fell, to push up the Malopo valley, through the Brickfields and into the south-east corner of the town.

The stout defence and heavy casualties convinced Cronje, in view of President Kruger's edict not to lose more than 50 burghers in taking the place, that such frontal attacks were unsustainable. And indeed apart from a making a half-hearted attempt against the kopje again next day no further major attacks were made against the defences by the Boers until their attack on 15th May 1900, two days before the town was relieved.

Despite the lack of Boer initiatives, Baden-Powell continued to maintain pressure against them. And on 3rd November the first attack was made on the Boers in the Brickfields. Captain Goodyear, who was severely wounded in the leg and had his thigh smashed, led the Cape Boys in a successful attack on the Boers in the Brickfields turning them out of a trench. As a result of Captain Goodyear's injuries, Corporal Currie, Cape Police, took over command of the Cape Boys,

## Attack on the Boer laager
The Boers had established a laager on the west side of town with about 250 men and two entrenched 12-pounder guns and a

one-pounder maxim with which they continually fired on the African stadt and the defences. It was strongly rumoured that the Boers were planning an assault against the stadt from this laager so Major Godley who was in charge of the western defences determined to try to pre-empt and dislocate the Boer attack and with Baden-Powell's blessing planned a night attack on the laager.

At 2.30 am on 7th November, Major Godley paraded his force. He had 60 men (dismounted) of the Protectorate Regiment under Captain Vernon with, mounted, one troop of Captain Cowan's Bechuanaland Rifles, and also two-pounders and a Hotchkiss gun under Lieutenant Daniel, BSAP. Captain Marsh's Squadron, Protectorate Regiment was held in readiness to support if necessary.

With Captain Vernon's troops leading, Major Godley moved his men to a position within range of the laager and as dawn broke over the veldt, he woke the Boers with shells and rifle fire. Surprise was complete; the Boers fled towards Cronje's camp. As they fled they met troops coming from Cronje's laager to form up for the proposed attack on the stadt. Thus reinforced, the fleeing Boers rallied and strongly counter attacked. Major Godley withdrew, having achieved his aim of disrupting the intended Boer attack. During the withdrawal an incident occurred when the Hotchkiss gun upset and broke the limber hook. Gunners Cowan and Gordon under heavy fire from the Boers' one-pounder Maxim, repaired the damage, righted the gun and got it under cover without receiving a scratch. Captain Vernon kept the Boers at bay, retiring by alternate troops. The Boers' fire on the whole was very wild which kept casualties down; Major Godley and four men were wounded. Major Baillie reported three large wagons flying the Red Cross flag coming out to pick up the Boer casualties. Again the Boers seemed to have lost heavily.

In all these incidents the Boers seem to have suffered a higher rate of casualty than the British. This can only be explained by the greater disciplined firing by the British troops; in almost every incident eyewitnesses tell of the enormous expenditure of ammunition by the Boers. One of the myths of the Boer war has been that all the Boers were sharpshooters and excellent shots having been brought up on their farms, hunting and handling guns from a tender age. At Mafeking this myth is demonstrably untrue. No doubt there were individual brilliant shots, as their sniping showed, but in battle, when it counted, their rifle fire was poorly aimed and inaccurate. On the other hand, the British troops for the most part having had only one month's training were able to control their fire much more effectively. The next incident, the attack on Game Tree Fort, could be said to be the exception to this rule but as events will show the casualties caused by the Boer fire were at point blank range when it was almost impossible to miss.

In mid November Cronje departed with 5000 men and many of his guns. He left behind General Snyman to continue the investment with between 2000 and 4000 men. In addition he left the Creusot Siege gun, "Creaky" and six other guns.

**The attack on Game Tree Fort**
It was Boxing Day evening when the newspaper correspondents were warned by Lord Edward Cecil, the Chief of Staff, to be ready at the Dummy Fort by 3.00 am to witness an attack that was going in on the Boer fort at Game Tree. This was a planned, deliberate attack on a Boer strong point about two miles north-west of the town from which, for a number of weeks, the enemy had poured on the British defences in that area 'persistent rifle and artillery fire'. According to Hamilton the attack was ordered for the purpose of 'breaking the cordon with a view to ultimately re-opening communications with the north'.

Captain FitzClarence's D Squadron and Captain Vernon's C Squadron Protectorate Regiment were detailed to attack from the east supported by the armoured train and 20 men of the BSAP under Captain Williams with a one-pounder Hotchkiss and a Maxim. Further support was provided by Captain Cowan and the men of the Bechuanaland Rifles, all under overall command of Major Godley. On the left, with Colonel Hore in overall command, Major Panzera had command of three seven-pounders and one cavalry Maxim with a troop of the Protectorate Regiment and two troops of A Squadron Protectorate Regiment under Captain Lord Charles Cavendish-Bentinck in reserve. Colonel Baden-Powell and his staff were, with the correspondents, to observe progress from the Dummy Fort, being directly opposite Game Tree and perfectly positioned between the two wings of the attack.

The attack commenced at 4.28 am with a bombardment by Major Panzera's seven-pounders. The effectiveness of this fire is questionable. Baillie reported seeing the shells 'burst merrily over the fort' whilst Hamilton who was also present in the Dummy Fort said the shells 'burst short or beyond Game Tree with no very striking effect'. The cavalry Maxim concentrated on the undergrowth, stretching about 60 yards from the left-hand rear corner of the fort, in which the Boer riflemen were concealed in pits and firing on the British left wing.

As they hoped that the guns would create a breach in the wall of the fort, the attack was left to Major Panzera's guns for about 45 minutes. But, unhappily, the damage to the fort was minimal and no breach was effected. Also, unfortunately, the Boers had removed rails so that the armoured train was unable to get in position to support the right flank as planned. Nonetheless, the attack went on; the men of C and D Squadrons advancing by rushes until about 200 yards from their objective when, led by their officers, they charged in the face of heavy fire from the Boers. Captain Sandford was the first to fall, mortally wounded but exhorting his men to go on; Lieutenant Swinburne took his place. The latter was one of the nine men of the Squadron who came out of the action unwounded. Then Captain FitzClarence was shot through the thigh and unable to continue. Captain Vernon who had been wounded in the advance was hit again but managed to reach the objective with Lieutenant Paton. They found that the Boers had made the fort impregnable. Lieutenant Paton and Corporal Cooke attempted to get onto the roof, but

## The campaign

found no way in through that route, the roof having been reinforced with steel. The entrance had been sealed and two tiers of loopholes had been built into the walls; Paton and Captain Vernon were reduced to firing their revolvers into the fort through the loopholes until they were killed. Bugler Morgan tried using his bayonet but he was shot twice in the legs. Others tried using their bayonets too but were shot down, until eventually the force was compelled to retire as Boer reinforcements were spotted riding to the scene.

The stretcher-bearers with Surgeon-Major Anderson, Dr Tom Hayes and Dr Hamilton and their team of dressers went out under the Red Cross flag to bring in the dead and wounded. With the truce, the Boers swarmed out of their trenches. They helped to bring out those who had fallen close to the fort as the British stretcher bearers were not permitted to approach closer than 75 yards and ambulances no closer than half a mile. The correspondent J. Angus Hamilton was able to visit the scene at this time and he reported discussing the attack with the Veldt Kornet in charge who praised the courage of the men who had carried out the assault. Hamilton also saw some of the Boers robbing the bodies of the dead and wounded. He remonstrated with the Boer officer who apologized but regretted that he was unable to control the younger, unruly elements of his command. In this connection it is reported that Bugler Morgan, who had had £3 and his silver watch stolen while he lay wounded, had, later that day, the items returned to him by a Boer orderly under flag of truce, while he lay in hospital.

The British casualty list was very demoralizing to the town. Nurse Craufurd in her diary called the day, 'the saddest during the Siege'. She reported 18 dead, including Captain Vernon, Lieutenant Paton and Captain Sandford and 30 wounded with two missing. The final casualty figures, because some of the wounded succumbed to their wounds, were three officers and 21 NCOs and men dead, Captain FitzClarence and 22 men wounded with three missing. The facilities at the Victoria hospital were swamped and so Baden-Powell asked Lady Sarah

Wilson with Nurse Craufurd to set up the convalescent home at the Railway Institute to look after patients who were moved out of the hospital to free beds for the new arrivals.

Much is made, in the reports of this fight, of suggestions that the Boers were forewarned of the attack, the implication being that the Boers had, therefore, reinforced the blockhouse and removed the rails on the night concerned and were waiting for the British assault. It is of course possible, that wind of an impending attack had reached the Boer authorities; there were a number of Cape Dutch living in the town whose sympathies no doubt lay with the enemy, and getting messages across the lines was relatively easy. But it seems, from what the Veldt Kornet told Angus Hamilton, that they had been on alert, anticipating a British attack, for several weeks. Also, the evidence that the newspaper correspondents, who were usually well informed about all that was happening in the garrison, did not know about this attack until they were invited to the Dummy Fort to witness it late on Boxing Day, seems to indicate that news of the plans had not got out. It is most likely that it was a well-planned attack on a target that turned out to be more heavily defended than anticipated. Possibly previous successes had made the garrison over-confident and led them to underestimate their enemy.

**Battle for the Brickfields**
The Brickfields, situated on the south-east of the town had not been included in the original defence line. Their proximity to the town and the fact that a number of kilns there provided ideal positions for observers and cover for snipers led the Boers to creep forward and build trenches and strong points in the area. By February their snipers were creating problems for the garrison and moves were made to counter the threat. The sector was held by Inspector Marsh and the Cape Police with the Cape Boys under Corporal Currie. The British in their turn built a system of trenches to counter the Boers, and in places these trenches lay 80 to 100 yards apart. Much ammunition was reported to have been expended on both sides with little effect.

Grenades made their appearance with the closeness of the trenches. Casualties, as has been said, were, thankfully, light, owing in no small measure to the use of steel plates with very small loopholes on the trench parapets. To keep the Boers worried, Baden-Powell used his megaphones at night giving orders loudly to imaginary troops to 'Fix Bayonets!' and to 'Charge!', which would always draw a response of wild firing from the Boer trenches.

Arrangements had been made for the Beleaguered Bachelors' Ball to be held on Saturday night of the 11th February, as the closest to St Valentine's Day. Unfortunately on that day Councillor Dall was killed so the Ball was postponed for 24 hours. On Sunday night the Ball was in full swing at the Masonic Hall with officers in their dress uniforms and ladies in their finery when at about 8.00 after the dancing had been going for about an hour a staff officer appeared and required all officers to report to their posts. The Boers had been spotted massing in trenches opposite the Brickfields and an attack was expected. The maxim was transferred in the dark—no mean task—to the eastern defences and the Bechuanaland Rifles and a squadron of the Protectorate Regiment were pushed forward to replace the Cape Police who had themselves been ordered to reinforce the extreme eastern outposts. The troops "stood to" all night, facing about 300 Boers who expended considerable quantities of ammunition. Baillie reported that 'Our men did not fire much'. By 6.30 am Monday morning things quietened down as no Boer attack materialized. The danger from Boer snipers had not however diminished and, sadly, Captain Girdwood, Customs and the Assistant Commissariat Officer, was killed later that morning as he mounted his bicycle in front of his house.

Little by little over the days and weeks of February and March by means of saps and counter-saps the British extended their perimeter driving the Boers from their trenches until, on 23rd March, the Boers withdrew from their strong point leaving it booby-trapped with several cases of dynamite left behind in the trench. The bomb was spotted and the British withdrew blowing up the trench on their departure.

These operations in the Brickfields although not producing dramatic military confrontations provided a series of morale boosting incidents for the garrison, which without doubt had had its confidence shaken by the debacle at Game Tree. They culminated in the withdrawal of the Boers and the extension of the perimeter. For the Boers on the other hand, confidence boosted by their success of Game Tree, the continual pressure and success of the garrison in pushing slowly forward, together with news of reverses elsewhere in the war, must have contributed to a sapping of morale.

**The final attack**
The final confrontation took place four days before the town was relieved. Commandant Sarel Eloff, who was President Kruger's nephew, was an ingenious and determined soldier. He joined the Boer forces blockading Mafeking with the express purpose of taking the place. He did not believe in its impregnability and for several weeks made a careful study of the defences to identify points of weakness. He had to assist him three deserters from the Protectorate Regiment from whom he obtained detailed intelligence on the layout of the defences. He decided eventually that the best point of entry was up the Malopo valley and through the African township, the stadt, from the west.

The attack was prompted by the closeness of the relief column; by the 12th May Mahon's troops had reached the Setlagoli River, 45 miles as the crow flies from Mafeking. If he did not act, Eloff realized, it would be too late; so in the small hours of the morning of 12th May, before the dawn, he arranged with General Snyman for a feint, an attack from the east side of the town. At about 3.15 am heavy rifle firing against the eastern defences commenced. The alarm bells sounded in the town and the defenders raced to their posts. Angus Hamilton reported that, '…very heavy fire was breaking out over the town from the main enemy position in the east. Gradually this fire was extended until the flanking positions of the Boers north-east and south-east were also engaged. As we stood to our arms... it seems they were directing an attack on the Brickfields'.

Meanwhile, Eloff and his advance guard of about 300 men, amongst whom was a party of foreign soldiers of fortune, were making their way along the Malopo riverbed into the Stadt. They were not undetected. The outposts in the face of such numbers were unable to do more than fall back on either side of the river to give flanking fire on the enemy. Major Baillie has suggested that, indeed, the attack was not unexpected and that a Maxim gun had been set up specifically to counter the threat, but on the night the gun had jammed. Eloff's plan was to secure the stadt and the BSAP Fort, the headquarters of Colonel Hore and the Protectorate Regiment. Once secured the Boer main force was to follow up and overwhelm the defences of the town.

On arrival in the stadt, to create panic and act as a diversion, one party of the Boer force began to fire the native huts whilst the remainder raced for the BSAP fort which they surprised and quickly captured along with Colonel Hore, Captain Singleton, Veterinary Lieutenant Dunlop-Smith, 15 NCOs and men of the Protectorate Regiment, Captain Williams and three men of the BSAP, and five native servants. The Baralong together with the men of the river outposts formed up behind the Boers and prevented the entry of the main body. By this time a defence had been organized

Baden-Powell, it seems, was not fooled by the feint from the east, expecting it to result in the usual half-hearted attack on the stadt. In his report of the action he wrote: 'four am on the 12$^{th}$ they opened a very heavy musketry fire on the town from the east, north-east and south-east... I therefore wired [signalled by telephone] to the south-west outposts to be on the look-out'. He had not, however, anticipated the scale of the penetration along the Malopo although he quickly recognized the danger and within 20 minutes 'order and confidence had been restored on our side' (in the words of Major Baillie). Clearly contingency plans had been laid for order to have been restored in so short a time.

The edge of the town facing the BSAP fort was reinforced and a defence line set up. The Town Guard, the Bechuanaland Rifles and the Railway Division were ordered to hold the railway line. Major Panzera with his guns together with Lieutenant Feltham's troop of C Squadron Protectorate Regiment took post at the railway bridge. The town itself was reinforced by men of the Cape Police from the Brickfields and by the British South Africa Police from Cannon Kopje Fort. Thus the Boers found their way into the town barred and unless General Snyman with the Boers' main body with artillery could force their way past the outposts now reinforced by the very angry, burned-out Baralong, Eloff's men were cut off.

At the BSAP Fort Commander Eloff demanded the surrender of Colonel Hore and his men. The position was hopeless. Colonel Hore and his men could not withdraw into the town and were heavily out-numbered and so with heavy heart he and the other 22 men in the fort laid down their arms at about 5.30 am and Eloff with a party of about 200 Boers entered the fort.

Meanwhile rifle fire from the town drove back Boers on the edge of the Stadt nearest to the Fort, preventing reinforcements reaching the men in the fort. This enabled Inspector Murray of the Cape Police and Lieutenant Feltham with his men to fight their way to this edge of the stadt clearly interposing a force between the stadt and the occupied BSAP fort. In the stadt itself, Major Godley with Captains Marsh and FitzClarence and the men of B and D Squadrons Protectorate Regiment fought a house-to-house action gradually forcing the Boers back until, shortly after midday, the Boers were divided into three parties, the largest in the fort, another of about 25 corralled in a mule kraal on Minchin's farm and a third, numbers unknown, still at large in the stadt. At the mule kraal, Major Godley surrounded the position on three sides and brought up Lieutenant Daniels with a seven-pounder to within a couple of hundred yards. He then called upon the men within to surrender; they refused and fought on bravely, holding Major Godley's men at bay for some time. Eventually, after pouring in some heavy volley fire, Godley's men charged with fixed bayonets; 25 Boers raised the white flag.

On the surrender of the 25 Boers in the kraal, Major Godley turned his attention to the Boers remaining at large in the stadt. He contrived to skirmish and drive back the enemy in the direction from which they had come, while Captain Lord Charles Cavendish-Bentinck with C Squadron Protectorate Regiment managed to interpose his men between the Boers and their escape. The enemy were hemmed in and caught in a crossfire. However as dusk was now falling and a number of prisoners already taken, and no doubt taking thought of the requirement to feed all the extra mouths these additional prisoners would represent, Major Godley ordered C Squadron to withdraw and permitted the enemy to escape.

At the BSAP fort, Colonel Hore and the prisoners included the *Times* correspondent, J. Angus Hamilton. He, hearing the shooting at the stadt and seeing the African huts on fire, had set out to visit the Fort at the local headquarters to discover what was happening. On his arrival, Hamilton found the Fort had been captured by the Boers. He was taken prisoner and placed with the others in a store that had been the Officers' Mess wine storeroom. It was small and dark and with the 27 prisoners from the fort plus Hamilton and three others, who were, like him, caught out, very crowded and noisome. Conditions were not helped by the fact that one of the men was suffering from dysentery. The prisoners spent the day not knowing what was happening. Bullets soon punctured the water tanks so there was little for either Boers or the prisoners to drink. The enemy turned out to be a cosmopolitan lot, French, Germans, Italians and Irish republicans as well as Boers. They quickly looted the place, the Boers, according to Hamilton being the main culprits: 'In the short time the enemy had been in possession of the Fort many of them had ransacked the premises, breaking open boxes, cutting open bags and generally appropriating all the effects that they found. It seemed to me ...the men engaged in this work were Boers'. The deserter, Trooper Hay or Hayes (authorities differ on his name) was reported by Hamilton to be seen swaggering around wearing Colonel Hore's sword and having a gold watch and chain hanging from his belt.

The requisitioning of the Children's hospital by Eloff has already been described, as have the visits of Nurse Craufurd to the prisoners in another chapter. The fight for the Fort went on all day. At one point a Frenchman, drunk from liquor looted from the officers' mess, climbed onto the roof shouting 'Fashoda' and waving a bottle. He was promptly shot and fell wounded. In the town Baden-Powell authorized the release of military prisoners from the gaol. These included Lieutenant Murchison held for the murder of Mr Parslow and Sergeant Major Looney who had been convicted of fraud. Both were issued with rifles and did their duty in the line.

Towards evening, after being subjected to very concentrated fire all day, it became clear that some one hundred of the Boers were attempting to break out despite the orders of their commander as they were seen to be shot at by their own side as they made a dash for the stadt. How many of these made it through the lines back to their own laagers is not known. Commander Eloff finally surrendered to Colonel Hore but the men in the fort had difficulty persuading the forces outside that this was not a trick and it took a lot of shouting by the ex-prisoners to get the attackers to cease fire. The Boers were marched out of the fort to hand their weapons over to the Cadets and then, as prisoners, they were taken under guard to the Gaol and overflowed into the Masonic hall. That evening in a chivalric gesture typical of the age, Eloff and two of his officers, Captain von Weismann and Captain Bremont were dined at Headquarters. Next day one of the German junior officers requested an urgent interview with the Chief of Staff, Lord Edward Cecil, to request to be released on the grounds that he was on leave from his regiment in Germany and that his leave was up and he was due back. It is not recorded what was said to him; needless to say he was not released.

1  *Times History of the War in South Africa* (Short title *Times History*) p. 80.
2  *Times History*, p.88.
3  See *Times History*, pp. 72–74 for details of the Boer Organization.
4  Stirling, p. 210.
5  J.A.Hamilton ,*The Siege of Mafeking*, (short title Hamilton) p. 58.
6  A.M. Craufurd, *A Nurse's Diary in Besieged Mafeking*, p. 61.
7  Casualties are difficult to establish accurately, since each side had an interest in minimizing its own and exaggerating the enemy's. In the case of this engagement it is of interest to see on a recent Internet page published by the town of Mafeking that the Boers claimed they had two killed and six men wounded having caused British casualties of four dead and 16 wounded.

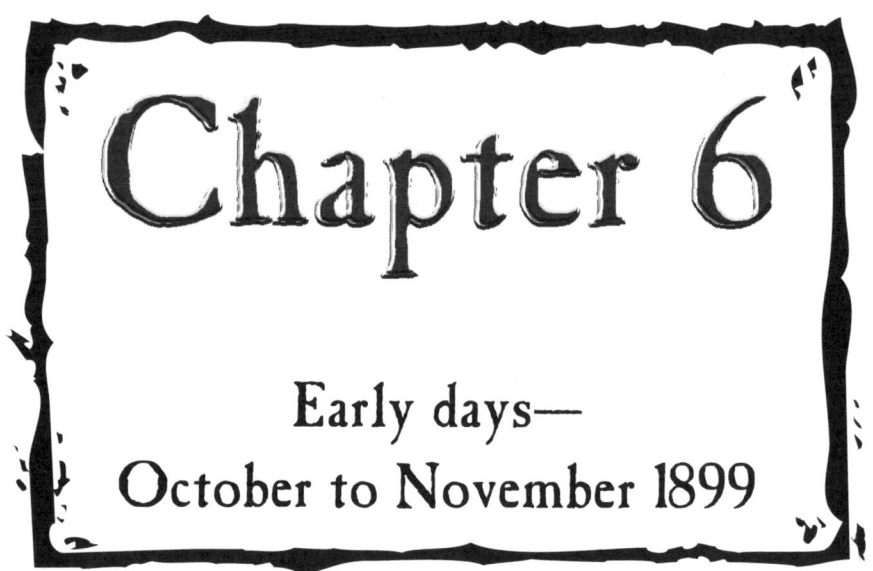

# Chapter 6

## Early days— October to November 1899

> *In consequence of the armed forces of the South African Republic having committed an overt act of war in invading British Territory, I give notice that a state of war exists.*

Part of the Notice proclaiming Martial Law, issued by Colonel Baden-Powell

A state of war existed between Britain and the Boer republics on the expiration of President Kruger's ultimatum at 5 pm on 11th October 1899. Two days before, Colonel Baden-Powell had issued a notice that was published throughout the town, ordering six alleged spies known to the authorities to leave town. Despite this a number of men, about 30, of Boer descent were rounded up and interned in the gaol on the day war was declared. These, it seems, were largely from among the refugees who had come in from the Transvaal in the days before hostilities. These refugees appear to have been accommodated on the north bank of the Malopo to the west of the town. Another group of about 300 refugees approaching the town on 13th October were mistaken for the enemy and fired upon, but they persisted in pushing through. They turned out to be African

### Early days—October and November 1899

workers from the Johannesburg mines. They were accommodated on the south bank of the river to the east of the town in what became known as "The Strangers' location". Many were recruited into the Black Watch under Lieutenant MacKenzie.

Friday 13th October saw the first shots fired. The armoured train was sent south to see just how far it was possible to travel; at about six miles it came upon a party of Boers in ambush. After an exchange of fire, described by Ross in his diary as, 'Opening the ball as far as the western Transvaal border was concerned'[1], the train returned safely. Also on the 13th, a truckload of dynamite was discovered sitting in the Mafeking sidings. It was rumoured in the town that the Stationmaster, an Irishman called Quinlan together with his "pal" Whelan, another Irishman working on the railway, had deliberately not forwarded this truck to Bulawayo because as Fenians and disaffected, they had intended blowing it up and the town with it. The truck was hitched to an engine and pushed northwards out of town until the driver, one Perry by name, spotted a party of Boers heading south along the line. He stopped, uncoupled the truck and then gave it a hard shunt in their direction. The Boers, believing it to be part of an armoured train, opened fire on the truck whilst Perry set his engine in reverse and headed back to town just as fast as he could go; after he had steamed about half a mile his engine was shaken by a tremendous explosion. It was rumoured in the town that the truck had created a 40-foot crater; at least two Boers were killed and a number were injured. Quinlan and Whelan were arrested and charged with High Treason and incarcerated in the gaol.

Early the next day the skirmish at Five Mile Bank took place where Captain FitzClarence and the Protectorate Regiment were engaged for the first time and did not disgrace themselves. The Boers, however, fired on the British ambulances that went out under the Red Cross flag to collect the dead and wounded. General Cronje later apologized to Baden-Powell, after the latter sent a letter under flag of truce to complain. This firing on the Red Cross flag happened time and again. Despite Baden-Powell and Cronje's representative meeting under a flag of truce on the 15th and agreeing that four places in the town, the Victoria Hospital, the Convent, Weil's store and the women's laager, flying the flag, would be spared bombardment, it often seemed that the flags were taken as a point of aim by the Boer gunners.

For the men of the defences, especially the Town Guard and the Railway Volunteers the first days of the war were exciting; it was all new, the manning of the redoubts and trenches, the night sentry duties, orderly duties carrying messages, the novelty of it all buoyed them up. Of course, the success of the initial engagement at Five Mile Bank did much to enhance morale. Being under bombardment was also a novelty, as Ross describes:

> '...not hearing the expected tremendous bursting of shells, I was for a few minutes undecided what to do, so got up and went out into the Court House compound to see what was going on. A man was on the roof of the Court and hardly had I recommenced (sic) speaking to him, when over our heads bang went the bursting of a shell. I picked up two or three of the pieces, when it struck both the man on the roof and myself that it was hardly safe to stand out in the open, so ...I hurried across to our bomb-proof cellar. The other man in the meantime had quickly done a slide off the roof and followed suit'[2].

At the Convent Sister Mary Stanislaus noted, 'It looked as if the Convent were the target, for shells were falling in the garden. Soon two crashed into the operating room changing it into a mass of splinters and dust [part of the Convent had been commandeered as an auxiliary hospital]. Fortunately the chloroform cylinder was untouched'[3]. The shelling ended at 2 pm

This first day of bombardment did little damage much to everyone's relief. Where the people of the town had expected destruction and death on a large scale they found, once the bombardment was over, there had been no human casualties at all. A chicken had been lamed by being hit by a piece of shell fragment, there were two holes where shells had entered the Convent and a window had been broken at the Mafeking Hotel. In Daily Orders Baden-Powell said, 'It will now be remembered that shellfire is more alarming than effective[4]'.

On 17th October the Boers seized the water works about one and half miles from the north-east of the town. This had no effect on the water supply in the town as all the old wells had been cleaned out earlier, in the month before the war, and new ones dug for drinking water. Water for other purposes was available from the Malopo River. Also on this day Colonel Baden-Powell sent the first of his famous "All well here" messages to the Chief Staff Officer, at Military Headquarters, Cape Town.

The first instance of the aggressive defence that Baden-Powell was determined to establish took place on 18th October after the town had been completely surrounded by the enemy. In the early hours a mixed patrol of the "Black Watch", Protectorate Regiment and Cape Police infiltrated the rear of the Boer position and opened fire at a range of about 400 yards. The Boers replied with wild firing and the patrol retired. After falling back for several hundred yards Private Stevens realized that Trooper Webb was missing. Stevens returned under heavy fire and found Webb lying on the ground having been shot through the ankle. Stevens then set about rescuing Webb, carrying him the two miles back to the hospital. For this action Stevens received a mention in Daily Orders.

The Boers tried the tactic of moving some of their guns closer to the town and shelling, until British guns were brought up forcing the Boers to retire. It seems they were astonished at how little effect their bombardment was having. General Cronje sent to Pretoria for a heavy Siege gun that arrived on 23rd October. It was a modern French Creusot gun firing a 94 pound shell with a range well in excess of anything the garrison had. It commenced firing, from an emplacement at Jackal Tree to the south of the town, on the afternoon of the 24th, firing two dozen 94 pound shells into the town. This gun was nicknamed "Creeky", spelt variously "Grietjie" or "Creechy", and given other names like "Big Ben" or "Au Sanna" by the Africans . Bombardment it seems had become the tactic favoured by the Boers to overcome the town's resistance. Frontal attack was ruled out because, taken in by one of Baden-Powell subterfuges, Cronje believed that the town was ringed with mines. It is likely that the explosion of the dynamite truck had had an influence on his assessment of the potential of mines. In addition he had had an instruction from his President, Paul Kruger, prohibiting any action that could result in more than 50 casualties.

The town's electrician, Mr Kiddy, was used by Baden-Powell to implement his "mining" of the perimeter. Kiddy went around the outskirts of the town in view of the enemy burying boxes with wires attached and marking out areas with little red flags. These red flagged areas were referred to by Baden-Powell in Daily Orders instructing the garrison to keep cattle clear of them as they were mined. While a small proportion of the buried boxes were live mines, many were just empty boxes. However, Kiddy was able to detonate one of his "live" mines on 26th October, blowing up an enemy ammunition waggon that passed over the top of it. This was a useful demonstration as it encouraged the Boers to be cautious. Cronje's telegram of the 27th to the Landdrost at Lichtenburg is revealing with regard to these mines: 'Yesterday... we systematically shelled the town... the enemy refused to surrender... I have received strict orders from the Government not to storm the town, because the place is protected by many minefields of lyddite and dynamite'[5].

On the 28th, Colonel Baden-Powell decided to take the initiative; Captain FitzClarence was sent out with his squadron of the Protectorate Regiment to drive the Boers out of a trench they had constructed half a mile east of town, rather too close. The night attack with sword and bayonet succeeded in driving the Boers out. After the British withdrew the Boers quickly re-occupied the trench but the psychological effect of this action lasted for a long time. It was not until March 1900 that the Boers finally abandoned the trench. As a result of this action and his actions at Five Mile Bank, Captain Charles FitzClarence was awarded the Victoria Cross.

It is difficult to reconcile the attack on Cannon Kopje on 31st October with President Kruger's injunction to minimize casualties and Cronje's orders not to storm the town. The answer probably lies in the frustration felt by the burghers at the lack of progress in taking the town coupled with indignation felt over FitzClarence's bayonet attack. These factors probably forced Cronje into authorizing the attack that was led by his son and in which his son died.

The attack on Cannon Kopje had a sad aftermath in the town. Lieutenant Murchison, of the Protectorate Regiment, who had been in charge of the seven-pounders, had dinner that evening with Parslow, a war correspondent for the *Daily Chronicle*, and over their wine Parslow began teasing Murchison about his shooting. This apparently went on for some considerable time until Murchison became very annoyed, telling Parslow to clear off. Murchison stormed out and went over to Dixon's Hotel, but Parslow wouldn't leave him alone, until, suddenly, Murchison drew his revolver and shot Parslow through the back of the head. Murchison was arrested and arraigned for murder. He was sentenced to death but this was commuted to life imprisonment by Lord Roberts, after the end of the Siege.

November opened with the start of the contest for the Brickfields which was to continue for the next four and a half months. Captain Flygare from the Scandinavian contingent with 20 of his men plus 60 burghers built a fort east-south-east of the town, close to the Brickfields. It was known as Klein Marico Fort, presumably because the burghers were from the Marico commando, or Fort Flygare. Two days later, on 3rd November, the Boers were digging trenches when Captain Goodyear, leading his Colonial Contingent, more commonly known as the Cape Boys, in an attack to turn the Boers out of their trench, was severely wounded. More generally during this early part of November the town came under heavy shelling and sniping. On 8th November, the day after Major Godley's attack on the Boer laager to the west, a shell landed on the Victoria Hospital, killing an African. On this day also, the Boers began the construction of a new earthwork 3,000 yards north of the BSAP fort. It was designated Game Tree Fort. Two days later, on the 10th, it was noted that shells were being fired from the position.

By the middle of the month, having had little to do but endure the constant shell fire, Mauser volleys and sniping, complaints and grousing amongst some of the troops in the Bechuanaland Rifles Volunteers and the Town Guard reached the authorities. Particulars of the Volunteers' complaints centred on the high-handedness and alleged bullying of their officer Captain Cowan and his summary dismissal of the popular Sergeant-Major Tiffin. The Town Guard, too, found the attitude of the Imperial or Regular Army officers hard to take[6]. It has to be remembered that many of these Town Guard members were the leading citizens of Mafeking who did not appreciate being treated, and ordered about, like private soldiers. A further cause for complaint, was what was considered the paltry sum of 2/6d per day allowance against the wear and tear of personal clothing. Ross writes: 'The Colonel [Baden-Powell] has today issued a notice to the town, stating that the authorities intend giving the Town Guard the magnificent sum of 2/6 per day, as an allowance.... and not as pay. So we are worth just 6d per day better than the native. How good of the Imperial Government who got us into this hole'[7]. Baden-Powell, it seems was compelled to issue further announcements regarding this matter stating that the sum granted to the Town Guard was in no way part of their pay packet but was recompense for the wear and tear to personal clothing while working in the trenches.

Rumours circulated everywhere, especially ones about the approach of a relief column, but one particularly nasty rumour had to be squashed by Baden-Powell himself. Mr Ben Weil, the storekeeper who had imported the massive quantities of food and stores that helped the town survive, wrote to the Colonel asking him to deny publicly a vicious rumour that was being circulated that he, Weil, and another man were getting up a petition to surrender the town. Baden-Powell was said to be furious and issued an order threatening 'dire consequences to any rumour monger'[8].

On 18th November, General Cronje handed over command of the Siege to General Snyman, and departed for the south with his forces of the Potchefstoom and Wolmaranstad commandos. Nevertheless, there was no let up in the shelling and sniping. Major Baillie thought that Cronje's departure might be a feint to lure the garrison into making a sortie but it seems he was genuinely under orders to move south.

By 22nd November the British authorities were concerned at the use, by the Boers, of the kilns in the Brickfields as sniping positions. A party, sent out at night to blow one of the kilns up, found it strongly defended and was forced to retire without completing its mission. With this setback an alternative means of attacking the enemy had to be found, and an advanced trench was constructed down to the riverbed, which brought the Boers in the Brickfields within about 600 yards range and the big gun within 1,400 yards. On the night of the 27th/28th Lord Charles Cavendish-Bentinck and his squadron of the Protectorate Regiment occupied the trench. During daylight of the 28th they fired volleys at the big gun every time they saw the Boers approach the position, with a consequence that no 94-pounder shells were fired at the town. Between times Lord Charles's men, supported by Corporal Currie and his men of the Cape Boys, kept up fire on the Boers in the Brickfields and eventually the Boers vacated the brick kilns. The next night, 28th/29th, FitzClarence's squadron relieved Lord Charles's and kept up the same pressure on the Boers, who managed only three wild shots from Creeky during the day. Much amusement was had, according to Baillie, observing the antics of the Boers trying to get near their gun. Overnight the Boers built a gunners' protection around the big gun, and the 30th saw the 'hottest day's firing we have seen for some time'[9].

In the days immediately before Kruger's ultimatum the Boers had been massing their forces along the western Transvaal border and refugees, both white and black, had been arriving in Mafeking. Having been driven from their homes by fear of the Boers it is unsurprising that the predominant impression from accounts of the times is one of fear. The lack of hard news, fear of capture and fear of bombardment are all themes that led to a general atmosphere of fearfulness. In the postscript to the first of her surviving letters Ada Cock says '…This house I have is out of town, so if the town is shelled I am safe here'[10] and again on 18th October after the bombardment had started, 'We hear Krongee has sent to Pretoria for a seven-inch gun; if so we can't hold out unless help comes'[11]. Despite the general apprehension, there was also a degree of excitement and initially a lack of appreciation of the controls imposed by Martial Law. On 23rd October Mr Algie, the town clerk, Mr Hampson and Mr Grayson were placed under arrest for undertaking an unauthorized military action. They had ridden out beyond the outposts to watch an artillery duel in which two of the town's seven-pounders under Lieutenant Murchison temporarily put out of action a pair of Boer seven-pounders. Algie, Hampson and Grayson were let off with a caution.

There were a number of lucky escapes from the bombarding shells. A Mr Wenham whose house was out of town and out of sight of the Boer gunners, considered himself safe there and so spent as much time as he could at home. Late in November he decided to go into the town; he had not been walking for more than a quarter of an hour when a shell from Creeky fell on his house demolishing it. On another day a big shell fell into Bradley's yard when there were a number of people about but no one was hit. Ross reports, 'The marvellous and almost miraculous escapes during the Siege are the theme of everyone's conversation'. The bullets seem almost to have been more dangerous than the shells, though with these too there were some miraculous escapes; a railway guard in the Railway Volunteers was shot by a Mauser bullet, the bullet entering his head at one temple and exiting at the other[12]. The man said he felt no ill effects and after a short time in hospital was discharged to convalesce.

Eventually, once the bombardment had started, it was realized how, by using dugouts and shelters during the worst of the shelling, casualties could be minimized. A sense of fatalism seemed to take over as everyone from soldier to wives and mothers came to accept that there was nothing to be done to influence matters. Ada Cock again, 'We are always getting scared; only now we don't scare. They seem to cry "Wolf" so often'[13].

Sundays were the days when everyone, men in the trenches and the civil population, could relax and 'recharge their batteries'. On Sunday 29th October, Ross wrote:

'Another day of rest, thank goodness, owing to the arrangement[14] that has been made between our Colonel and the Boer General that no fighting should take place on Sunday. This enables the men at least to get a weekly wash, and set things out for the coming week... the women and children came out from their laager and it seemed like old times'[15].

In 1899 Guy Fawkes night fell on a Sunday and, after warning the Boers that explosions and coloured lights in the town that evening did not presage an attack, November the 5th was celebrated in traditional fashion providing entertainment as well as a link to pre-war and better times for the population. It was an important psychological boost at a time when the shelling was still a new and unnerving experience for most. Another celebration that left a few sore heads was St Andrew's day, 30th November, which the Scotsmen in the garrison celebrated in traditional style.

First signs of caution over food supplies appeared in November on the 15th when an audit of the stocks of mealies, yellow mealies, sorghum and flour held by individuals, was taken. Partial rationing was introduced together with restrictions on the sale and purchase of alcohol. Ross grumbled, 'Talk about the rights of citizenship, why they have even stopped us getting our ordinary every day stimulants'[16]. The authorized ration was 1lb per man per day of bread, meat and vegetables.

The investment of the town was not so complete that runners could not get in and out. These were mainly Africans who carried correspondents' reports, military dispatches and letters. The first official dispatch from the outside arriving Thursday 9th November, bringing news of Elandslaagte and raising the spirits of the garrison with a belief that relief would not be long in arriving. The following Sunday the garrison had a welcome reinforcement by Sergeant Matthews BSAP and five troopers who had made their way from the north and broken through the cordon. Then, on the 15th, a Reuters dispatch rider, an American named Pearson, managed to elude the Boers and entered the town bringing news of Kimberley and that troops were arriving in the Cape from England. Two days later he departed together with a Mr Hellawell, the correspondent for the *Cape Times* who left without the permission of Colonel Baden-Powell, and who was captured by the Boers. Pearson successfully eluded the Boers again, calling on Lady Sarah Wilson at Mosita on his way south.

It is more difficult to discover African attitudes to the Siege. There were three separate groups of Africans in the town area, the largest group was the Baralong, the local tribe, who lived in the stadt. There were the Fingos or Mfengu who had settled in Mafeking some ten years previously living in a separate township on the south bank of the Malopo. Finally there were about 1,000 refugees[17], of mixed tribes but mostly Shangaan living in the refugee camp known as The Strangers location. This was sited between the stadt and the Fingos' village, to the west and adjacent to the railway. There is some evidence that Colonel Baden-Powell tried to exclude the Africans from combat, probably to protect the Baralong who were living elsewhere under the Boer administration from reprisals by the Boers. As a part of this policy the Baralong were not issued with firearms, although those that had their own were permitted to keep them and they certainly used them to defend their homes, by manning defences along the lower slopes of Cannon Kopje to the west of their stadt.

There is just one source of contemporary African opinion, the diary of Sol Plaatje, a Baralong who as an educated man, held a highly privileged position for an African. By the nature of his employment as Court Interpreter, he was far from the herdsman, subsistence farmer or domestic servant that made up the majority of his fellow Baralong. As Plaatje's diary only starts on 29th October and ends in March 1900, we do not, therefore, gain his impressions of life for an African when Martial Law was first declared nor do we hear of the final weeks of the Siege and of the relief.

Bullets and shells are no respecter of persons, and the Baralong were as angry as any at having their homes shelled. Just as the Boer gunners sent their shells into the women's laager so they fired their guns at the stadt. It may have been a deliberate policy to attempt to demoralize the population, perhaps to encourage the blacks to rebel against the town authorities and demand a surrender. If it was it failed; it just made the Africans angry. Sol Plaatje tells that, when on 7th November African volunteers were called to accompany Major Godley on his attack on the Boer laager, 80 men stepped forward keen to go out and capture the big gun. However, on hearing that this was not the purpose of the expedition, the majority declined to join and Plaatje says only 20 Africans actually participated[18].

The Fingos seem to have been employed largely as herdsmen, but they would also go out at night to raid the Boer cattle; on 24th November they staged a large raid but were unsuccessful because, they reported on their return, the Boers had not forgotten FitzClarence's bayonet attack and were very alert.

It was largely the refugee Africans from the mines in Johannesburg, who were used to pick and shovel work under white supervision that were initially employed in the digging of trenches, dugouts and defence works. Although Plaatje wrote on 28th November, that a shell burst among a party of Baralong working on the defences killing one and seriously wounding two[19], these may have been the defences of the stadt. In the early days a great deal had to be built because the town authorities would not permit large-scale defences to be constructed until war was inevitable. It has been suggested that although the whites all had shelters and bomb proofs dug for them the Africans failed, or were too fatalistic, to appreciate the need for underground protection even after shells began to land in the stadt.

As the town settled down to a routine, if still dangerous existence, by the end of November the newspaper correspondents were finding it harder to find exciting stories to file. Vere Stent, Reuters' correspondent, accused the Principal Medical Officer, Dr William Hayes, of operating on Africans without anaesthetic, a charge vehemently denied by Dr Hayes. He issued a circular calling for Stent to substantiate his claim or to publish a retraction. He also banned the war correspondents from the hospital. They complained to Baden-Powell who considered the whole thing rather childish. The hospital being now a military hospital and subject to Queen's Regulations the Principal Medical Officer could not ban the correspondents from the building. Baden-Powell wrote in his Staff Diary 'The whole correspondence was childish... the treatment of Africans in the hospital was all it should be'[20]. But this kind of thing was to be expected; the strain was beginning to tell, with small incidents taking on an exaggerated significance in the minds of those, who like the doctors, were most under stress.

---

1     B.P.Willan, *Edward Ross—Diary of the Siege of Mafeking*, p.17 (short title Ross *Diary*).
2     Ross *Diary*, p.24.
3     http//www.mafikeng.co.za—Mafeking Web site for extract of Sister Mary Stanislaus Diary.
4     A.Renew, Chronology of the Siege.
5     J.F.Midgley, *Petticoat in Mafeking*.
6     Ross *Diary*, p.47.

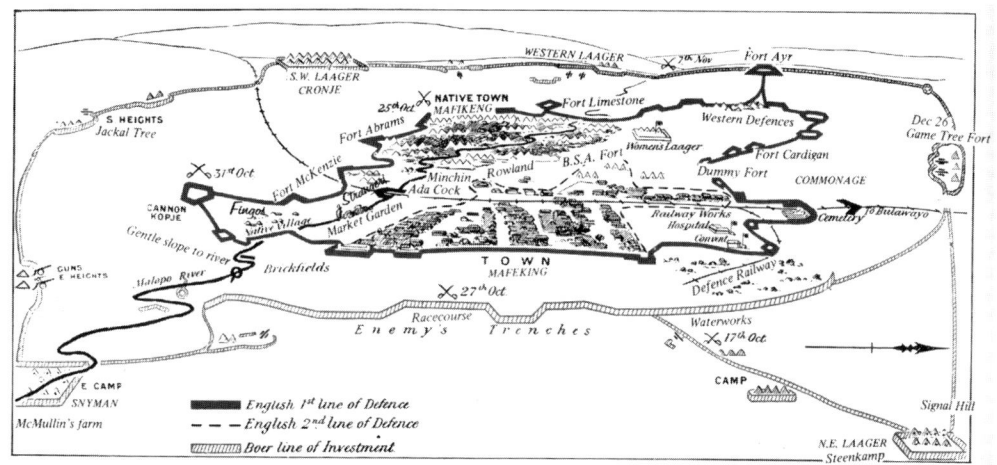

**Top:** Topographical sketch by a British officer showing the British and Boer positions in mid-November 1899, brought by a runner to Bulawayo.

**Bottom Left:** This picture of Boer commandos shows the varying age ranges – here three generations.

**Bottom Right:** Medical treatment of the wounded on the battlefield.

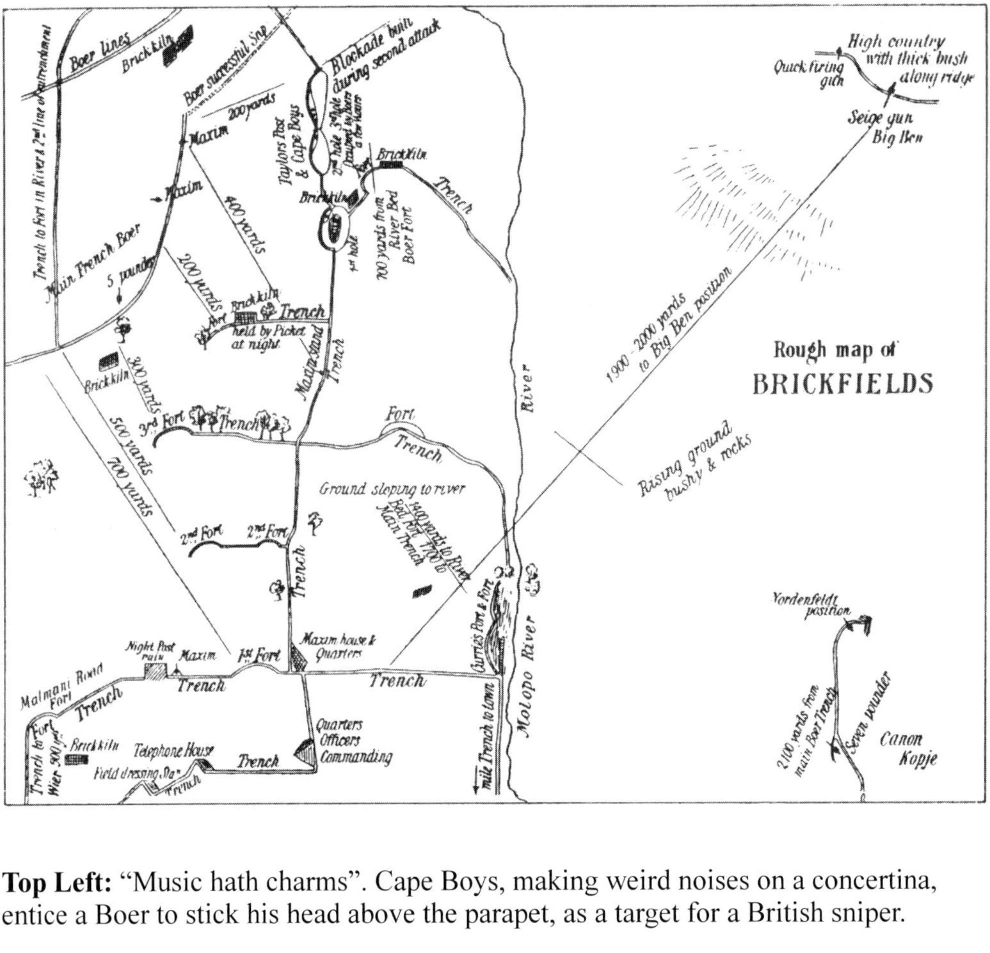

**Top Left:** "Music hath charms". Cape Boys, making weird noises on a concertina, entice a Boer to stick his head above the parapet, as a target for a British sniper.

**Top Right:** Boer spies on the way to prison.

**Bottom:** Rough map of the Brickfields.

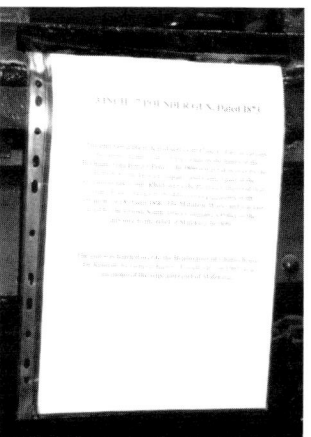

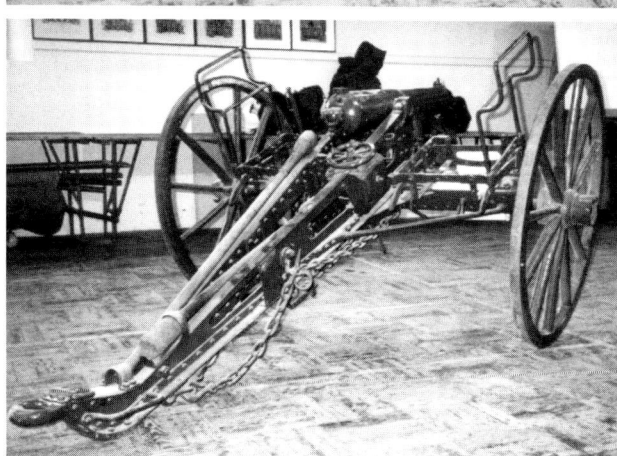

**Top Left:** The history of the "Mafeking Gun" as appears on the gun today in the Charterhouse armoury.
**Top Right:** The Western outposts; bird's-eye view of the Native town.
**Middle:** The "Mafeking Gun", presented to Charterhouse School in 1907 by Baden-Powell. The gun is an 1873 3-inch 7-pounder and was used in several campaigns, being last deployed by the BSAP in their advance to the relief of Mafeking.
**Bottom:** The "Mafeking Gun", a different perspective.

**Top:** The co-author Edmund Yorke, with the "Mafeking Gun".

**Bottom Left:** A Mr Cohen's house is destroyed

**Bottom Right:** The effects of the Boer shells.

**Top:** Some of the gallant defenders. From Left to Right: Lt Daniel, guns; Insp Harvey, Cape Police; Capt Cowan, Bechuanaland Rifles; Lt Feltham; Lt Wellman; Lt Pechell; Capt R.J. Vernon, KRR (killed Dec 28); Maj A.J. Godley; Capt F.C. Marsh; R.W. Kent; Lt H.P. Paton (killed Dec 28); Capt H.C. Sandford, ISC (killed Dec 28); Lt Holden.

**Bottom Left:** Major Godley's attack. Lieutenant Paton's trench prepares to fire a range of 1,500 yards, 7.30 a.m.

**Bottom Right:** Some of the gunners who took part in Major Godley's attack.

**Top:** One of the seven-pound guns used during the Siege. In the background is a section of shrapnel – damaged corrugated iron roofing salvaged from the Mafeking Club.

**Middle:** The two seven-pounders used during the Siege. One is dated 1873, and the other 1876.

**Bottom:** One of the seven-pound guns used during the Siege.

**Top Left:** The "Lord Nelson" muzzle-loading ship's cannon, dated 1770. During the Siege it was discovered being used as a fence post, and pressed back into service.

**Top Right:** The "Lord Nelson".

**Bottom:** Shells and shell fragments from the Siege on display in the Mafikeng Museum.

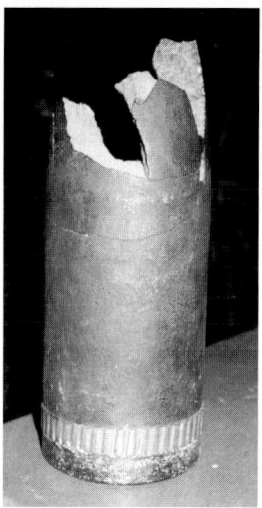 

**Top Left:** Long Tom shell fired from "Old Creechy", also known as "Old Creaky". This shell was found in the early 1970s by the Museum Curator, Audrey Renew and was on display for a long time before an expert noticed that it was "live". It was exploded in the veld and Audrey collected most of the fragments and glued it together.

**Top Right:** The Union Jack which flew over Dixon's Hotel.

**Bottom:** Shells and shell fragments from the Siege on display in the Mafikeng Museum.

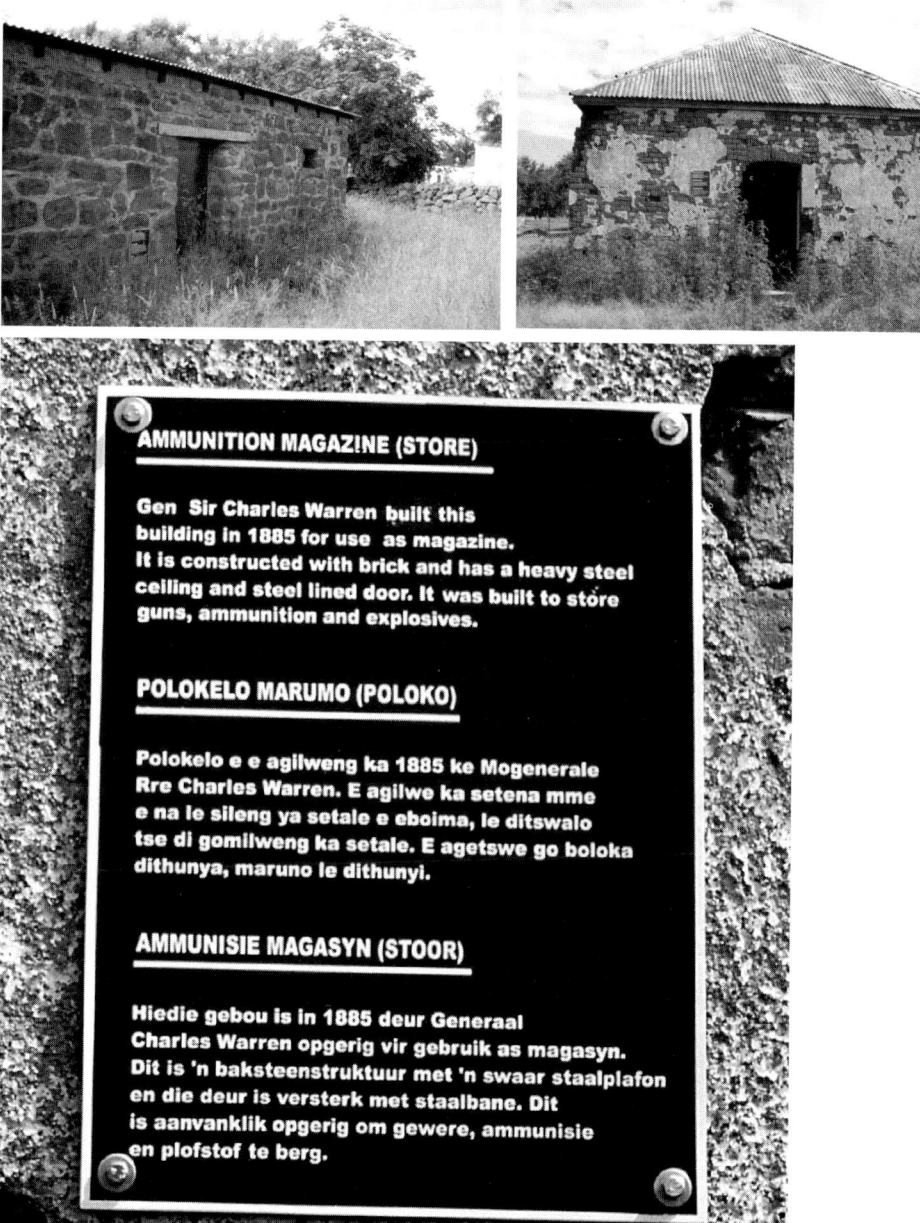

**Top Left:** Warren's Fort at the old BSAP barracks. It was in this fort that Veldcornet Eloff held out until forced to surrender after his pre-dawn attack on 12th May 1900.

**Top Right:** The ammunition magazine at the old BSAP barracks.

**Bottom:** The ammunition magazine at the old BSAP barracks. Close-up of the information board

**Top:** The Mafikeng Museum, which was the old Town Hall, built just after the Anglo-Boer War.

**Bottom Left:** A portrait of Solomon Plaatje.

**Bottom Right:** A contemporary drawing of Dixon's Hotel.

**Top:** Mounted Maxim gun at Cannon Kopje.

**Bottom Left:** Major Lord Edward Cecil.

**Bottom Right:** Colonel Plumer's attempt to relieve Makeking.

**Top:** One of the Boer forts outside Mafeking.

**Middle:** Some of the Boers besieging Mafeking. General Cronje (later captured at Paardeberg), whip in hand, stands at the breech of the 94-pounder Long Tom "Creechy".

**Bottom:** Mafeking's artillery. On the left is the "Lord Nelson" and next to it is "The Wolf", the little howitzer made in the town.

**Top Left:** Colonel Baden-Powell in Hussar uniform.

**Top Right:** Lieutenant Smitheman, of the Rhodesian Regiment, managed to get through the Boer lines and returned with reports for Colonel Plumer.

**Bottom:** The Baralong chiefs. Seated center is Wessels, with Melema at left and Lekoko at right. The tribe's headmen stand behind.

**Top:** The women's laager.

**Middle:** A Boer trench outside Mafeking.

**Bottom Left:** A mounted orderly sounds the stand-to bugle call in front of Dixon's Hotel. The cyclist orderly prepares to deliver orders. The building on the right is Colonel Baden-Powell's headquarters.

**Top:** A truce on the Game Tree Hill battlefield. Curious Boers crowd round the British wounded.

**Bottom Left:** Lady Sarah Wilson in her dugout.

**Bottom Right:** Robert Stephenson Smyth Baden-Powell as a major-general.

**Top:** Artillery in Mafeking waiting to link up with the relief column.

**Middle:** The procession through the Market Square after the relief.

**Bottom Left:** The meeting of Baden-Powell and Mahon.

**Bottom Right:** The first train into Mafeking. Note the foliage-camouflaged wagons at right.

## Early days—October and November 1899

7   Ross *Diary*, p.50.
8   Ross *Diary*, p.51.
9   Major F.D.Baillie *Mafeking—A Diary of the Siege* (short title Baillie) p.55.
10  Midgley, *Petticoat in Mafeking*.
11  Midgley, *Petticoat in Mafeking*.
12  Ross *Diary*, p.56
13  Midgley, *Petticoat in Mafeking*
14  An agreement was made on the first Sunday of the Siege between Baden-Powell and Cronje at the Boers' request that there should be a truce on the Sabbath.
15  Ross *Diary*, p.35.
16  Ross *Diary*, p.50.
17  There is some doubt over numbers as most authorities including Baden-Powell suggest 1,000 whilst Willan in a footnote states 2,000.
18  Willan and Reed, *Mafeking Diary*—Sol T. Plaatje (Short Title Plaatje), p.29. Entry for 6 Nov.
19  Plaatje, *Mafeking Diary,* p.39.
20  Baden-Powell's Staff Diary—National Army Museum.

## Chapter 7

### Christmas under seige—December 1899

*If these hours be dark at least let us not sit deedless
like fools and fine gentlemen.*

William Morris

There was only one major military event during December—the British attack on Game Tree Fort on 26th, and that turned out to be a disaster. The month started relatively quietly for the town with what was considered to be only light shelling. This may have been due to a Boer shortage of ammunition. By the start of the month the advanced trenches in the Brickfields were up to the Boer saps and Baden-Powell had to restrict the use of ammunition by the Cape Boys who were being too enthusiastic in their volleying and expending cartridges at an unacceptably high rate.

The practice was for a troop of the Protectorate Regiment to be brought into the town at night to act as a reserve in the event of an attack. The troop slept in the Court House, leaving to march back to their own lines just before dawn. On 6th December, at that time, and just before the men were "fallen in" to march back, the Boers fired heavy volleys down the street in front of the Court House

## Christmas under siege—December 1899

where the men paraded. Happily the Boers were just too early to catch the troop, but their timing made folk wonder about how such detailed information on troop movements had reached the Boers. The same trick was tried by the Boers five days later, this time as the soldiers arrived at the Court House, but again their timing was just a little slow, and all the soldiers were inside by the time the volley arrived.

On the 11th Colonel Baden-Powell tried to sow dissension in the ranks of the Boers, by sending out a proclamation under the white flag to all their camps. He addressed it to the burghers individually, pointing out that any Boer victories achieved so far had been against only the 'advanced guard of the British force...The main body of the British is now arriving by thousands from England, Canada, India and Australia, and is about to advance through your country'[1]. He then went on to say that the burghers should think of their farms and families; he warned of the destruction of their farms by Africans,

> 'Your leaders have caused invasion of native territory, and looting of their cattle, and have thus induced them to rise and in their turn invade your country, and to kill your burghers.... Yesterday I heard that more natives are rising, and are contemplating similar moves...Thus great bloodshed and destruction of farms threaten you on all sides...my advice to you is to return without delay to your homes and remain there peacefully till the war is over...'[2].

This proclamation with its offer of amnesty was reportedly written in extremely bad Afrikaans creating a degree of amusement amongst the burghers who could be seen gathering in clusters by the townspeople who were not privy to what was happening, and were bemused by the number of white flags that had been seen heading out to the Boer lines. Snyman was reportedly furious by this attempt to suborn his troops. He sent in a strongly worded note to Baden-Powell demanding that any further communications for his burghers be passed through him.

On the 17th Baden-Powell tried another ruse, it being a Sunday and therefore no fighting taking place, and the burghers having every opportunity to observe what was happening in the town. Thirty men were picked and mounted on the fittest-looking horses. They were given 'lances with pennants' (really pointed sticks used for tent pegging with ribbons attached) to carry and made to ride around to various points on the perimeter and show themselves, giving the Boers the impression that a reinforcement of lancers had slipped through their lines into the besieged town[3].

Over the period of the 16th, 18th 19th and 20th a number of artillery duels took place that resulted in the Boers being driven from trenches as well as their five-pounder being put out of action by the shooting of Captain Sandford with one of the old seven-pounders.

The rainy season was now in full spate and most days of the month record at least one downpour, much to the discomfort of the men in the trenches, the most spectacular of which is reported in full below. However, there were numerous other miserable days for the men in the line, such as Thursday 28th when it commenced raining hard during the night and continued all day. 'All the trenches were washed out and in some parts of the sniping trenches the men were standing up to their waists in water. It was impossible… for them to move, and not by any chance able to get out, their being too close to the enemy'[4].

On the 5th December, a quite unprecedented storm broke over Mafeking. Its effects can best be described by an eyewitness, the *Times* correspondent, J. Angus Hamilton:

> '… shortly before noon, clouds were bunched high up across the sky and over the Boer laager. From where we were in the town it was quite apparent that the temporary centre of the storm was almost above the emplacements of the enemy's artillery. Before the breeze had increased the Boers had thrown a few shells into the town, but presently, as the force of the gale struck us, it was evident that the

rain-filled clouds were discharging their contents ... For an hour or two the Boers received the full effect of the storm, and but few drops of rain fell into the town. The deluge quickly left the south-east, concentrating a little beyond and over the town, and seemed to have deserted the Boers. The veldt was quickly flooded, the dried-up spruits were soon charged with foaming cataracts, Mafeking itself lay under water, the earthworks around the town were swept away, trenches and bomb-proof shelters were choked with eddying streams, everywhere was ruin—destruction and complete chaos reigned until the storm had spent itself[5].

Down Cannon Kopje there rolled:

'the surging tide, carrying in its might the stores of the fort, the blankets of the men, the bodies of struggling animals, which, if they succeeded in coping with the force of the stream, were dashed to pieces upon the rocky facing of the hill. The women's laager, which has hitherto rested in snug seclusion at the base of the hills forming the western outposts, was, in a few minutes, flooded with the off-pourings from the sluits of the veldt, while the trenches were quickly submerged or silted with the refuse of the torrent. In the town, bombproof cellars were vacated, and the people, discarding their shoes and stockings, made their way from point to point by paddling and fording the footpaths across the streets. To the north of the town, below the exterior outposts, the men stripped to the skin, allowing the full strength of the streaming downpour to beat upon them. The Market Square was a sheet of running water, rising with such rapidity that it seemed that the houses bordering the square would be inundated. From Market Square, upon two sides, the roads make something of a descent, and down these slight inclines volumes of water, yards in width and some feet in depth precipitated themselves to the riverbed. As the storm increased it was seen that it would be impossible to retain any longer our advanced positions in the riverbed. The first to go was the trench occupied by Corporal Currie and his African sharp-shooters. As the water swept from bank to bank through this post, which we, but a few days before, had won so gallantly from the enemy, the men clambered up the banks to the veldt and made their way as best they could to the base. With the flooding of this position, so rapidly did the river rise, that those occupied by Captain FitzClarence and his squadron were equally untenable. As they were abandoned the stream rushed by them with the roar of a river in flood. Within an hour the river had risen eight feet, and so unexpected was the flood that for the time being it was not possible to rescue from the rising stream the seven-pounder gun, which was in position some way down the river'.

As the rain continued the wind died down, until in the height of this storm it scarcely possessed the strength to dissipate the white mists that were rising from the veldt. They hung low upon the ground, prevented from rising by the strength of the downpour, and making it difficult to see the progress of events in the enemy's lines. From time to time above the hissing of the rain and the roar of the rivers we heard the angry cough of the Nordenfeldt, the shrieks of their quick-firing guns, and the heavy and more stately boom of "Big Ben".

The area of the storm included the most advanced trenches of the Boers, and:

'As the wind shifted the gloomy masses of vapour we saw through the whirling mist, the Boers, rain-soaked as ourselves, standing disconsolately upon their muddy parapets. They did not seem to understand what they should do... These men, themselves, stood still, shaking the water from their limbs, attempting to dry their weapons'[6].

During the night, under cover of the darkness, the garrison and townspeople rebuilt their defences.

The next day, the 6th, Mr Gerrans the local waggon builder, who had made a name for himself extracting the explosive from unexploded Boer shells, (it seems there was a large proportion of their ordnance that failed to explode), was using a drill on a 94-pounder shell with two of his workmen when it blew up. Mr Gerrans and the workmen were injured whilst a passer-by, Mr Smith of the Town Guard, was hit by a piece of the casing and killed. Mr Gerrans cannot have been too badly injured as, later in the month, he was building the carriage for the old ship's cannon discovered on Rowland's farm being used as a gate post[7].

On 7th December arrangements were completed for the exchange of Lady Sarah Wilson; she was swapped for Viljoen, a horse thief held in Mafeking gaol and wanted by the Boer authorities. The opportunity was also taken to exchange a Dutch couple, who had entered as refugees and been held prisoner in the town, for the Cramonds, a railway couple captured by the Boers at Pitsane to the north of Mafeking. Also on this day an unfortunate event occurred outside Lennons Chemist Shop in the Market Square; a 94-pounder shell ricocheted off the square, struck an African, taking off one of his legs and an arm and mortally injuring him, before smashing through the window of the shop and exploding inside. Moments later another shell ploughed through the other window of the store, exploding and narrowly missing five people still in the shop. Sadly one piece of this shell entered the hotel bar next door, killing Corporal Franklin who was having a pick-me-up after dealing with the injured African.

Tradesmen were directed on the 12th to disclose details of all their stocks of eatables; liquor was not included as there was still a plentiful supply. On the 20th it was decided that the meat supply should be augmented by any animal killed by shellfire or other enemy action

Dr Smyth refused to treat the women in the women's laager on the grounds that they couldn't pay. He was only prepared to handle private patients who paid his bills. Other doctors seem to have been more ready of offer their services on a basis of need. Dr F. Hayes was the town's Principal Medical Officer operating at the Hospital with Surgeon Major Anderson. Dr Tom Hayes looked after the women and children in their hospital, set up at the end of the month. Surgeon Major Dowling looked after the military Field Hospital set up by the bridge over the Malopo. Unfortunately on 17th December Dowling fell heavily off his horse, 'and was badly cut about'. This accident put him out of action for some time.

Rumour was rife, especially about the approach of the relief column, although by this time not many believed that they would be free by Christmas. On the 22nd a runner found a way through with a copy of the *Bulawayo Chronicle* which astounded everyone as it ran a story of a major battle on the Malopo River and the relief of Mafeking by a column from Kimberley. The story caused much amusement; it was thought that the writer had misplaced the fight on the Modder River to the Malopo River!

Sundays became more and more important in the lives of the garrison and Baden-Powell went to ever-greater lengths to encourage competitions and to engage people in the sports and entertainments. Christmas Day was brought forward to the 24th as this was a Sunday and there was no knowing if the Boers were going to extend the truce to Monday 25th. In the event they did. On the 24th there was a children's party hosted by Lady Sarah Wilson. About 250 children were conveyed from the women's laager by the Protectorate Regiment, members of which competed for the best decorated and turned out rig—won by Captain Vernon who was killed two days later at Game Tree Fort. In the evening Lady Sarah and her husband hosted a dinner for Baden-Powell and his staff, Ben Weil reportedly supplying a turkey that had somehow been overlooked! For others there was a lavish dinner laid on at the Mafeking Hotel. Ross noted 'the menu was really a remarkable production considering the complications surrounding and their inability to get what was required. A very pleasant evening was spent'[8].

The next day, everyone having done their celebrating the day before, was very quiet. The men in the trenches overnight had to contend with a severe hailstorm which had washed some of the trenches away. The officers of the Protectorate Regiment held their Christmas dinner at Dixon's Hotel apparently, again, with a really good spread. Unusually for the times, Lady Sarah was present as a guest, especially as her husband was not an officer of the regiment. It was not common practice in those days for the officers of a regiment to invite ladies to join them at dinner. It seems that Mr Whales, editor of the *Mafeking Mail*, threw a party for many of his friends in the town at which the whisky flowed, as did the patriotic songs.

The gaiety of the Christmas truce evaporated with the disaster of the Boxing Day attack on the Game Tree Fort. Whether or not the Boers were informed of the day and time of the attack, which is unlikely, there were certainly some indications that something was afoot. Ross noted in his diary on the 22$^{nd}$ that 'We are daily expecting to hear of Baden-Powell issuing orders for a night attack as all the men of the PR [Protectorate Regiment] have been served out with india rubber shoes'[9]. Given the known movement of Africans across the lines it is unsurprising that the Boers were ready for the assault on the 26$^{th}$.

The old naval gun discovered by Major Godley earlier in the month was tried out with a "home-made" round shot on the 28$^{th}$ from Limestone Fort. The gun had been reconditioned in the railway workshops by Messrs Tarplay, Scully and Murray and set on a carriage built by Gerrans. The result was very satisfactory—the solid shot was reported to look exactly like a cricket ball as it rose in the air. It landed just short of the Boer laager about 3,000 yards away and then bounced and ricocheted through the camp. Boers were seen to be alarmed by this new weapon; they hitched up their wagons and moved farther away, which is probably why the gun acquired the reputation of having a range of 7,000 yards.

An insight of the dangers faced by the African couriers is provided by Plaatje at the start of the month, when he tells the story in his diary of a dispatch rider called "Freddy No.2" who, looking for a way past the Boers, called at a mission station at Kuruman to ask directions for the safest route through the lines. There he found the missionary, a Reverend Brown, who was flying the Vierkleur (the Boer Flag). The Reverend Brown refused to assist "Freddy No.2" and sent him away as soon as he realized that he was trying to get into Mafeking. Nevertheless "Freddy No.2" made it into the town with his messages, but was arrested by the Boers as he attempted to leave. They took him to Vryburg, arriving late at night, and whilst the Boers were reading the dispatches they found on him, "Freddy No.2" escaped. Returning to his village, he was not recognized the next day when his pursuers arrived at the village and called upon him to act as interpreter when they questioned the chief.

The Baralong cattle were an important source of meat for the town and the African herds were still being watched over and guarded in the traditional way by piccanins (small boys) despite the herds being grazed on what was disputed land between the British and Boer lines. Everyday the cattle would be driven out to graze and brought back at night. It was dangerous work as the herds were often the target of the guns and the herd boys too were sometimes shot. In November a goatherd had been killed as he tended his herd behind the hospital. During the first week of December the Boers tried to set up a fort opposite the stadt, apparently in an attempt to try to limit this grazing, but the infuriated Africans kept up such a fire on the structure that the Boers abandoned it. Herd boys afterwards crept up to the abandoned structure and returned with some loot in the form of biltong (sun dried meat), tins of bully beef and a couple of spades.

On another night, on 9th December, two herd boys crept up to the Boer Camp under cover of the darkness and the rain and watched as some Boers were outspanning their oxen from their carts. Because of the wet, the Boers were in a hurry to get under cover so, leaving their oxen yoked, they tied them up and went inside. The herd boys managed to untie two yoked pairs and bring them back to Mafeking. On arrival back at the British lines, the herd boys were met by members of the Black Watch on sentry duty who, according to Plaatje[10], tried to claim credit for the capture of the oxen themselves. Colonel Baden-Powell was called in to adjudicate and by virtue of the fact that the two Baralong boys could produce the riems (leading reins) he decided in their favour. The authorities permitted the Baralong to retain one of the oxen while purchasing the other three from the boys. Plaatje's story indicates a degree of friction among the various African communities in the town.

In a reprisal raid the next day the Boers tried to steal Baralong cattle as they were being driven out to graze, but were held off by Cornelius Gaboutloeloe, the organizer of the Baralong cattle guards. Just as his bandolier was almost empty a number of men came to his aid and the Boers were driven off, but not before they had wounded one man and three cows.

Not all raids on the Boer cattle were so successful. Plaatje reported that on 22$^{nd}$ December two Bangwaketse went out at night to steal sheep. They were driving 'their flock' through the Boer lines when one of the sheep let out a bleat alerting the Boer sentries who opened fire; only one of the pair made it back to the British lines, without, needless to say, the flock[11].

On the question of African involvement in the war, Baden-Powell wrote a somewhat disingenuous letter to Snyman on 8$^{th}$ December[12] suggesting that the Africans really wanted to be neutral between the two nations, British and Boer, but that the behaviour of the Boers towards the Africans had driven them to take up arms against them and the Boers had only themselves to blame if they were attacked by the Africans. One point of interest arises in this letter, Baden-Powell uses the term "wireless telegraph". What he meant by this term is not clear. Whilst a primitive form of wireless telegraphy, with a range of about 60 miles, had been used in Navy manoeuvres in 1898[13], there is no record of Mafeking possessing such equipment. This must, therefore, have been yet another bluff on Baden-Powell's part.

Life for the African population at this time had not yet seriously deteriorated. Plaatje reported that a civil action brought by 14 employees of the Julius Weil Stores, the local representative of which was Ben Weil, against their employer Julius Weil for unpaid wages was heard by the Court of summary jurisdiction set up by the Military authorities in the town. The court found in favour of all the plaintiffs except one[14]. An African wedding, (unfortunately we have not been given the names of the bride or groom), took place in the English Church according to Ross: 'The bridegroom's friends with rifles and bandoliers formed a guard of honour'[15].

Danger still lurked though, and shells and snipers continued to take their toll of the African population. The poor boy who was hit by a shell outside Lennons Chemist shop has already been mentioned; Hamilton reporting the incident said that he was very stoical, just saying, 'Boss, Boss, me hurt' when the stretcher bearers were carrying him off[16]. In a similar incident a week later, when a shell landed in the stadt a woman had both her legs removed by the ricocheting projectile.

With all the men called up and spending much of their time in either the trenches or in shelters when off-duty and with wives away in the women's laager, houses and businesses in the town were unoccupied for long periods. As many homes were damaged by shells and were consequently insecure, there was an obvious danger of looting. So the death penalty was imposed to deter looters. On 20th December a looter was sentenced to death by the court; he was reported to have been convicted of theft previously and ordered out of the town and not to return to Mafeking on pain of death. The man apparently failed to take the warning seriously and returned to be caught again and executed.

By the end of December life was taking on a pattern for everyone in Mafeking; people were coming to accept the death and destruction that were their almost daily fare. Sundays had become the focus of their week, a day when the township folk could escape from their bomb-proofs and the Africans in the stadt and locations be sure that there would not be any heavy shells falling on them. Baden-Powell was very sensitive to the strain of living under the bombardment and provided ever-greater efforts to ensure that the Sunday holidays provided as much relaxation as possible. Throughout December rations were more than adequate and there was even enough for Christmas feasts and parties. The impression one gains from the records of the time is that, despite the set-back at Game Tree, virtually all the people of Mafeking looked forward to the new century with expectation and hope.

---

1   Baillie, p. 75-77.
2   Baillie, p. 76.
3   Ross *Diary*, p. 72.
4   Ross *Diary*, p. 81.
5   Hamilton, *Siege of Mafeking*, p.148.
6   Hamilton, *Siege of Mafeking*, p. 149-150.
7   Hamilton, *Siege of Mafeking*, p. 166.
8   Ross *Diary*, p. 76.
9   Ross *Diary*, p. 75.
10  Plaatje, *Mafeking Diary*, p. 53.
11  Plaatje, *Mafeking Diary*, p. 63.
12  Plaatje, *Mafeking Diary*, pp. 50-52.
13  The Concise Universal Encyclopaedia.
14  Plaatje, *Mafeking Diary*, p. 58.
15  Ross *Diary*, p. 68.
16  Hamilton, *Siege of Mafeking*, p. 142.

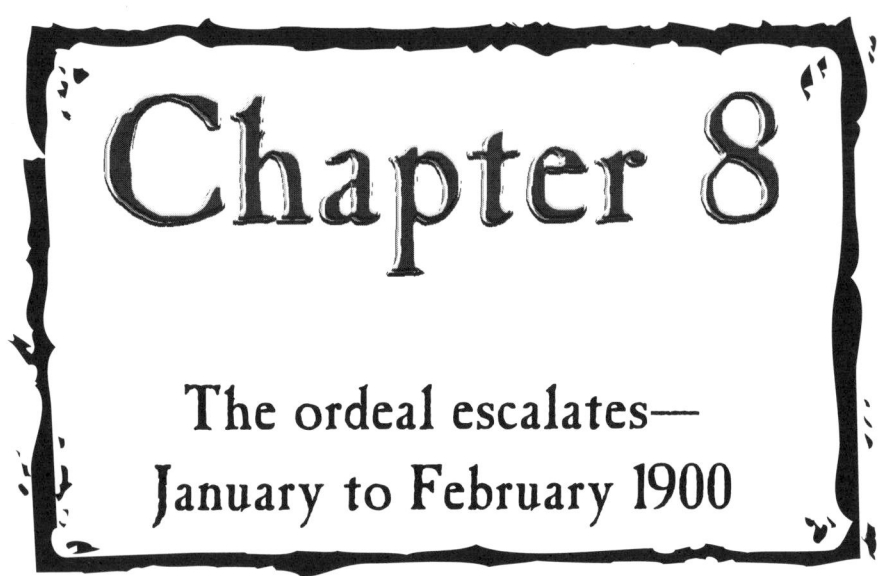

## Chapter 8

### The ordeal escalates— January to February 1900

*Another shell burst in the south... we wonder how long this is going to last. Instead of getting brighter, the prospect in front of us is darkening itself. I am inclined to believe that the Boers have fully justified their bragging, for we are citizens of a town of subjects of the richest and the strongest empire on earth and the burghers of a small state have successfully besieged us for three months—and we are not even able to tell how far off our relief is. It is certain that it cannot be too near.*

Sol T. Plaatje, *Mafeking Diary*
3rd January 1900

It was during the months of January and February that the full rigours of the Siege became apparent to the Mafeking inhabitants. In the wake of the extremely demoralizing Game Tree disaster and the news of the British reverses of Black Week during December 1889, military pressures on the garrison increased. As if to "rub in" their Christmas victories, Boer gunners celebrated New Year's Day with a vengeance. Mr Algie, the Town Clerk, counted 21 shells fired from Old Creechy that day, together with 40 smaller ones as well as those from a one-pounder maxim gun[1]. At times the shelling could be brutally indiscriminate. Ross noted how, on 3rd January, 'nearly all the shells landed in or about the women's laager, one shell bursting in the midst of some little children, killing one and mortally wounding another'[2]. Another morning, as Nurse Craufurd was busy in the hospital, 'washing my patients—shell after shell—94-pounders—passed overhead. I ran out sometimes to see where they were falling and every one—nine—went into the women's laager'[3].

By 20th January Big Ben had fired over 800 94-pound shells'[4]. Such heavy bombardments could result in horrific injuries. On 24th January a Big Ben shell killed one and severely wounded six native women in the Stadt[5]. On the 2nd January, Plaatje reported how another shell from Old Sanna hit the east of the stadt and 'amputated an employee [of Ellitson the butcher] in a most piteous manner—both legs and both arms'[6]. The flimsy defences of the shelters provided little protection against such a "monster". On 1st February a 94-pound shell struck one of the splinter-proof sheds at Cannon Kopje 'killing one man [Knox] who was really suffocated before he could be got out, breaking another man's [Francis's] leg and badly wounding another's back [T. Goddard]'[7]. Another 94-pounder, 'cut Councillor Dall, Sub Commandant of the Town Council, in half… the first townsman of any standing to be killed since the start of the Siege'. Mrs Dall was left 'prostrate in grief'[8].

Boer tactics varied considerably with the artillery guns regularly moved to different firing positions at all times of the day and night. In February new incendiary shells were fired adding to the terror of the Mafeking inhabitants. Sniper attacks deploying the dreaded long-range Mauser rifle constituted the other most feared tactic by the Boer enemy. Again, shooting could be callous and indiscriminate with all ages and sexes falling victim to this often terror tactic. One poor woman, named Poulton was 'shot through the head by a Mauser bullet' as she served her husband's dinner[9]. Some Boer sharpshooters became familiar figures to the garrison. On 15th January it was noted how 'an elderly Boer sniper nicknamed "Old Grey Beard Moses"' had been again hard at work with his "ping-bom" (Mauser rifle) 'ever since daylight this morning'[10].

The defenders replied with a mixture of tactics—artillery duels, counter-sniping and forays against enemy sniper and gun positions and trenches. Meanwhile, scores of new shells and fuses continued to be ingeniously constructed in the Mafeking home-made arsenal or factory. Much of the sniper activity continued to take place in the Brickfields area where front-line trenches were barely yards apart and "territorial rivalry" high. On the 19th January, for instance, Major Baillie reported, 'an artillery duel between one of our seven-pounders whose shells were made at our own factory here, and the fuses designed by Lieutenant Daniels, BSAP, in which the shells proved a complete success—the enemy's five-pounder... was almost immediately silenced'[11]. Lord Nelson, the ship's gun, continued to shoot with 'great violence' despite its 'doubtful precision'[12]. One successful foray on 1st February, reminiscent of World War I trench tactics, involved Major Panzera and Corporal Currie, who 'crept up to the nearest kiln from which the Boers were, unfortunately, absent and had blown it up with 50 pounds of dynamite'[13]. Baillie also recorded a highly successful 300-yard sniper duel which is highly illustrative of the nature of fighting in this "sniper's paradise" and worth quoting in full.

> 'One Boer who for some extraordinary reason wore a white shirt (which he will never do again) occasionally showed his back over the edge of a shelter he was constructing for himself, acting apparently on the principle of the ostrich. Trooper Piper of the Cape Police eventually got him and at the same moment, his friend, who was firing from the loophole, fired at Piper; fortunately Corporal Currie CP, who was covering the loophole, fired almost simultaneously and got him too, to the huge delight of the Cape Boys. The second man was a bearded man and a well-known sniper—he was an excellent shot and the news of his

demise was recorded with unusual pleasure by the garrison'[14].

By the end of February such steady attritional tactics had resulted in at least one significant military success—Fort Cronje, an important Boer sniper post, was captured enabling the meagre British artillery to shell the Boer positions at Game Tree Fort comfortably.

For both blacks and whites enduring the Siege of Mafeking, the most serious indication of a growing crisis was the steady onset of stringent food rationing. Already in November as we have seen local corn supplies had been commandeered and Ross observed on 9th January how the authorities were now 'taking over all grocery stocks held by the merchants and townspeople' with many things now beginning to run low—no oatmeal, matches, milk, tea, etc and... worst of all whisky'[15]! By the 11th 'all tin stocks' had also been commandeered by the military. Baden-Powell encountered some entrenched white and black opposition to these measures as penalties for hoarding or price exploitation became progressively stiffer as the weeks passed by. A major target for Baden-Powell was the leading European merchant, Weil, whose demands for a rise of ration prices in early January by 7½p rested on claims of a significant loss of profit. Baden-Powell's view was less than sympathetic; 'I find that by loss he means inability to make the enhanced profit essential to the Siege... I have declined to raise the price'[16]. The most outstanding European example of profiteering was the case of the perhaps aptly named Sergeant-Major Looney who was arrested by the Commissariat officer, Captain Ryan, for 'selling stores to townspeople', one sack of wheat illegally sold by him from government stores accordingly found in a Mr Moore's bedroom! On 18th February when Looney made a full confession of theft from the government stores, Baden-Powell angrily recorded: 'On hearing that I intended to have him shot'[17]. Instead, on 20th February, Looney was sentenced to be reduced to the ranks and five years penal servitude as well as discharge with ignominy, pending an appeal to the Commander-in-Chief. Plaatje recorded the tense situation in the courtroom and the subsequent public humiliation of this officer:

'Major Godley was presiding, and all the others present were dressed in their best uniforms. The Court was crowded and I left it still in progress... Looney was arraigned on the market square and sentence was promulgated by Major Godley. According to the newspaper on Tuesday, we were allowed to be present at the promulgation. He was sentenced to be reduced from the ranks of His Majesty's Service and to serve five years penal servitude ... he was handed over to the civil powers. I felt so sorry for him—such a pretty young fellow. I understand that he has a wife and child'[18].

Penalties for African offenders were also harsh. One Alfred Ngidi, already dismissed for being asleep whilst on sentry duty, 'came in for a very rough time. He appeared again this morning on a charge of failing to hand over a bag of Kaffircorn. The sentence of the Court: seven days' hard labour and the confiscation of the Kaffircorn. Hard luck on poor little Alfred'[19]. African elite groups were also by no means exempt. Next day, 6th January, a dozen or so of the location people including the prominent, Lumata, and Mfazi, (Baralong) families, were arraigned, 'to answer to a charge of having wrongfully, unlawfully and maliciously neglected to hand over their grain when requested by the authorities to do so'. As Plaatje noted: 'Things are getting very serious'[20].

Specific grain stores were set-up by Captain Ryan, the ever vigilant Commissariat officer 'where each native was given a number on a metal badge' to ensure that they 'buy a ration at one particular store'. The military authorities, however, remained unnecessarily suspicious of the ways in which Africans disposed of their rations complaining that, 'if we issue Kaffircorn we find the natives at once make beer and sell it'[21]. It was a suspicion to a large extent based on their ignorance of the African diet. As Plaatje noted, it was a misunderstood viewpoint: 'It came to their notice that some Baralongali (sic) were selling Kaffir beer the other day. They look upon it as wasting... they do not know that Kaffir beer to a common Barolong is "meat, vegetables and tea" rolled into one, and they can subsist entirely on it for a long time'[22]. Baden-Powell himself soon became aware of African unease over these somewhat harsh policies. 'Baralong natives in the Stadt are getting a little suspicious of us. They want to know... why we are trying to take all their grain from them'[23]. As January progressed other European and Asian small traders became the particular targets of "food raids" as 'a good deal of meal etc was being kept undeclared by small traders and... unauthorized bread was being baked and sold illegally'. On one night raid a whole waggon-load of mealies was discovered, hidden away by Indian traders, the goods being confiscated and the owners duly tried by the Court of Summary Jurisdiction[24].

As military and social conditions deteriorated in this way, Baden-Powell was forced to exercise even tighter political control over the garrison. Baden-Powell became particularly suspicious of the alleged nefarious activities of members of the Dutch community within the garrison population and these groups, and also individual Africans accused of spying for the Boers, faced harsh penalties. It was noticed how Dutch women and children 'never moved out of their trenches' during the shelling which suggested that they were well informed by outside intelligence of forthcoming attacks. Dutch women in the women's laager were also suspected of communicating intelligence to their outside Boer kinsmen about the garrison's defences. On 27th January Ross noted how 'the spy business has now got BP's back properly up... moving all the Dutch women and children and some men out of the jail so that if the enemy do again attempt to shell our women they will kill their own friends'[25].

Three African spies were eventually executed during the duration of the Siege after trial by the Court of Summary Jurisdiction. Thus, on 28th January Ross recorded in his diary

'Native spy shot today by the Cape Boys at a distance of ten paces. Three bullets going through the head and three through the chest, the force of which drove him backwards instead of falling forwards into the grave'[26]. On 25th January Baillie recorded full details of this same case of 'a native convicted as a spy... he had been sent in to obtain full information as to the stores, forts, their garrisons, and the general disposition of the forces of the town. He quite acknowledged the justice of his sentence, but only seemed to think that it was hard lines that he should be executed before he had time to procure any information at all'[27].

During this period, censorship of the press was also significantly tightened and Baden-Powell took stern measures against both black and white citizens for seditious or treasonable talk. One interesting case was the arrest of the popular townsman, J.W. de Kock, for "working against imperial interests". This measure was seen as excessive, especially as the citizen himself was known for his loyalty. The men of his fort even produced a petition to seek his release on bail. Ross, a close friend of De Kock, was incensed by this example of the growing, unchecked powers of the authorities. 'What a power these autocrats have. They do just as they please in every matter, great and small, even to the liberty of the subject, without having to give the slightest reason why or wherefore'. He ominously noted: 'The imperial authorities must take care they do not raise a hornet's nest about their ears'[28]. Under such pressures there were also on occasions, mutinous mutterings within the garrison military contingents. Thus, on 1st February the BSAP men in one fort complained at, 'not being treated fairly by being left up there all the time of the Siege and that they should be relieved and changed to different positions'. More serious was the rising rate of desertion. On 25th February, for instance, Baden-Powell, angrily noted 'two deserters—out for ride—never returned—Boer and German'[29].

To control the majority black population within the garrison Baden-Powell took pains to construct an elaborate pyramidic hierarchy of social control. As in other colonial societies a network of black collaborators was sustained and rewarded with payments in cash and kind. At the top of the political hierarchy created were the chiefs and leading councillors of the Baralong, all of whom received generous allowances or "salaries". The chiefs played a vital role in grain requisition. Thus, Plaatje noted how grain from the stadt was 'always carried away by the chiefs... The officers are under the impression that when the chiefs reach a hut they take away the last crumbs they find in possession of the owner who would henceforth survive on what they purchase economically'[30]. When these African elites proved unreliable or troublesome they were swiftly replaced. The most notable event in this respect was the deposing, in January 1900, of the Baralong paramount chief, Wessels, and his supercession by the leading councillor, Lekoko. This major event in terms of Baden-Powell's political control and manipulation of the indigenous black population has been glossed over by most of the diarists who generally refer to the reasons for his dismissal as "drunkenness" or "serious incompetence". Hamilton, however, provides both a striking account of these proceedings, a politically tense moment in which Baden-Powell firmly stamped his authority on the local African elite, and the real (political) reason for Wessels's deposition. Wessels had, in fact, directly defied the authorities by 'instigating his tribe to refuse to work for the military authorities here, and through his instrumentality' it had, 'become difficult to obtain native labour and native runners'. He had preached sedition, 'telling them that the English wished to make slaves of them and that they would not be paid for any services they rendered; nor would they... be given any food but left to starve when the critical moment came'[31].

Hamilton noted how this was an 'interesting meeting... one which recalled the early days of Africa when the authority of the Great White Queen was not a power paramount in the council chamber of the tribes'. There was some significant resistance. Hamilton observed how, at the news of his supercession 'the old chief snorted with disgust and endeavoured to coerce his people to reject the demands made upon them. While the majority of the "Khotla" [African Council] attending the "indaba" [meeting] sided with the imperial authorities represented by the Civil Commissioner, Mr Bell', Hamilton noted how the, 'younger and more turbulent... spoke at once in an angry chatter and were inclined to express sympathy'[32]. In the event this significant confrontation between the local imperial authorities and the key African elite was safely executed with Wessels significantly being placated by the promise of a continuation of his allowance. He was, however, to remain a significant black critic of imperial policies during the remainder of the Siege.

Equally, if not more important, were the armed black military who, as we had have seen, played a crucial role in the Brickfields fighting. Mr Algie noted the four groups of 'armed native defenders' who constituted a privileged African class enjoying superior rations and equal pay with their European counterparts. These included the 60-strong Cape Boys 'made up of the coloured or half-breed servants, storekeepers and gardeners living and working in the town; Fingos, under Mr Webster; a detachment of Baralongs under Sergeant Abrahams and the Black Watch a composite group including a number of Fingo and Zulu tribesmen controlled by Lieutenant MacKenzie'(a European)[33]. All were to play an increasingly significant role especially during the ensuing three months of the Siege. The issue of deploying armed blacks remained a controversial subject and continued to be the focus of angry correspondence between the Boer Commander, Snyman, and Baden-Powell but particularly the Boer authorities, who were acutely aware of the implications for white rule and social order in general if this practice became too widespread. In January and February Snyman again accused Baden-Powell 'of arming and employing natives against us' to which Baden-Powell again replied denouncing such hypocrisy and noting again how Snyman was already deploying, 'an armed native watch solely for the purpose of catching our natives who are sent to steal cattle'[34]. The dangers of a wider multi-racial conflict emerged at another "indaba" with the newly appointed chief, Lekoko, who over-demonstrated his loyalty to his new master by proposing more active armed black participation in the conflict and requesting 'more rifles and ammunition and permission to strengthen his outworks'[35]. It was a request swiftly but firmly refused by an alarmed Baden-Powell.

Another significant, albeit unarmed African collaborative group were the "trench diggers". During January, night parties of between 300 and 400 African trench diggers, including already skilled refugee mineworkers from the Transvaal trapped within the garrison, completed a veritable maze of trenches around the besieged town. On 11th January, for instance, Ross noted the 'stupendous' work on the trenches... 'Of course the authorities have paid them for work done but where on earth should we have been without the assistance of their manual labour... It is a great credit to their loyalty and should be recognized by the Imperial authorities'[36]. Again, in organizing and recruiting trench workers the newly appointed tribal elite led by Lekoko played a key role—'no more loyal and deserving men could possibly be found than Lekoko or Silas Molema, the acting Chiefs of the Baralong nation'[37].

Another vital group to the survival of the garrison were the African runners, scouts and messengers. Under enormous pressures they daily brought in vital intelligence news reports and messages from the approaching relief force and neighbouring besieged garrisons. These tasks were often carried out at the cost of their own lives if not gross maltreatment when captured by the Boers, "punishments" ranging from flogging to mutilation. Thus, on 7th January Baden-Powell cryptically recorded in his staff diary, 'Our runners sent out north and south last night failed to get through Boer outposts'[38]. On 29th January Ross reported on what came to be a routine tragedy as one native despatch carrier was 'shot by Boers' and also a 'native woman had her breast cut off for the same offence'. For he and others these Boer atrocities confirmed 'what ghouls and murderers these great unwashed hogs are'[39]!

From the logistical perspective an increasingly important African group were the "nocturnal" and mainly Baralong cattle raiders who plundered Boer herds and farms outside the perimeter of the garrison. In the words of Hamilton, 'if sniping be the rule by day, cattle raiding by night gives to the natives some profitable employment'[40]. On 17th January, for instance, Ross paid tribute to the 'Mafeking Baralongs' who were 'doing more very useful work... having brought in... 18 head, and then another of 22'. He confirmed 'it would take a very long time to starve at this rate'[41]. Their food supplies were becoming vital. Thus, Baden-Powell had recorded the satisfaction in early January how 'two natives brought in 40 sheep' and later on on the 15th he confirmed, with delight, how, 'our native scouts brought in 18 head of fat cattle looted from the Boers'[42]. Hamilton went even further in his praise considering such Baralong raids of 'unique value in the garrison... the rich capture which these natives have made has given us a welcome change from bone and skin to juicy beef'[43]. As we shall see, even greater successes were to be achieved during the closing months of the Siege, the raiders themselves benefiting from a proportionate system of bounties and rewards of stolen cattle that, undoubtedly, were to help stave off the worst effects of the later food shortages.

For Baden-Powell it was essentially a "carrot and stick" system of political control. When not preoccupied (as he often was) with securing the defences of the garrison, he continued to devote considerable time to morale building. After the Game Tree debacle and with news of British military reverses during Black Week, Baden-Powell took great pains to raise the spirits of the garrison. It was a task for which the extrovert Baden-Powell, with his renowned gifts for amateur dramatics, was exceptionally well suited. As before Christmas a huge variety of entertainment was organized, mainly at weekends, to raise the overall morale of the garrison. On Sunday 21st January, for instance, an 'Agriculture and Produce Show' was organized, including 'stalls displaying vegetables, fruit, sewing work and knick-knacks made from shells, bullets, etc'. A particular highlight of the show was the prize awarded for the 'best Siege baby'[44]. Mr Algie recorded a typical if literally more "action-packed" entertainment weekend organized on the 11/12th February in which Baden-Powell played his usual prominent role.

> 'The Cycle Sports were cancelled on account of the rain the day before... a cricket match was played between FitzClarence squad and the Town XI. In the evening the Beleaguered Bachelors' Ball was held but the evening was interrupted by rifle fire. Men were called to their posts although the band played on till midnight. Baden-Powell gave two turns as "Senor Paderewski" and as "Gentleman Joe"'[45].

The European women in the garrison played a crucial role in these events, Lady Wilson recording, for instance, 'many Union Jacks to be made—a most intricate and tiresome occupation' and these were distributed among the various forts'[46]. The military and civilian diarists of the Siege paid fulsome tributes to the value of these events that, in Baillie's words, 'go far to relieve our spleen and vary the interminable monotony of the Siege'[47]. The tension could be relieved in other ways. The garrison was both heartened by, and marvelled at, the frequent displays of sang-froid in the face of the many near misses that occurred amidst the incessant rain of enemy shells and bullets. One noted how Major Panzera 'takes the biscuit for coolness' when a shell struck the ground immediately behind him as 'he was walking across the square. All he did was to slew around ... swing his fly whisk at the spot' and 'walk on quite unconcernedly'[48]. Another miraculous escape occurred as a massive Boer shell passed through the rooms of the Town Hall narrowly missing several groups of men (Mafeking volunteers) playing cards in groups[49]. The Siege ladies demonstrated similar stoicism, with Lady Wilson experiencing the 'narrowest escape ... that it is possible to imagine', as a shell struck a room in the Convent within 'four feet from where we were sitting'[50].

Such morale-building events could not disguise the embryonic signs of starvation within the African population. Despite rationing, by the end of January, Ross, for instance, recorded

> "I am very sorry to say the natives in the Stadt are having a very hard time of it. Scarcity of food amongst them, coupled with dysentery and other diseases... is carrying off large numbers. They even now come with their sixpences and tickeys (a colloquial term for the South African three pence coin) all over the town trying to buy peaches, however green they may be on purpose to get a square feed. This alone, I think is sufficient to feed the microbe of dysentery almost to the extent of it becoming a pestilence'[51].

Plaatje was already noting the potential for distress amongst the more recently arrived homeless and vulnerable 'miscellaneous collections of natives from Jo'burg who thought that the war would last a month or less. They came here as they thought Mafeking was safe enough to spend the month, after which they would return to the revolutionary Rand. They... include Pondos, Shangaans, Barotse, Zambesians and South Central African breeds'. They were a:

> 'harmless lot of people—some of them live under the two trees in the space between the BSA Police Camp and the stadt. They do a night's toil when they require a little cash to buy grain that they "nona" with horse flesh. They are quiet and are waiting for the end of this trouble and I am sure they would not do any harm to anybody'[52].

As rationing for both blacks and whites tightened in February, several diarists noted further signs of deterioration amongst *some* African groups. After bread was reduced to 6ozs per man per diem, with women receiving 3ozs and children 1½ozs, Ross noted how, already, the natives were, 'beginning to look a bit dicky on their half a pound of meal per day'[53]. On 6th February, a further key indicator of the beginnings of acute starvation occurred in town when a horse was killed by one of the Boer 94-pound shells. 'The moment the horse was dead the carcass was set upon by a horde of natives who, like a lot of Aasvogels [vultures], pulled and cut off the meat and carted it away until there was not a scrap to be seen. Some of them have had a good meal today at any rate'[54]. The horse's name was "Whiskey" and, in fact, belonged to Court Interpreter, Plaatje, who registered his shock at witnessing the terrible fate of his beloved horse at the mercy of this ravenous crowd: 'When I got there I saw only his blood and nothing more of him and a good thing too. A lot of Basutos congregated on the spot and hardly gave him time to die—so much in a hurry were they of getting his meat'[55]. By 10th February military eyewitnesses also confirmed the potentially dark disaster now looming. Major Baillie thus observed: 'The question of food supplies for the native had become very serious'. Presumably, with the continuing success of cattle raids 'it was not,' he confirmed, 'the question of meat so much as the question of grain'[56].

On 19th February the authorities took major steps to deal with the mounting food crisis as 'a soup kitchen was opened for the natives for the first time' and '800 rations of soup were served out'[57]. Such was the success that 'several other soup kitchens were to be opened in different sections of the town'. Horseflesh soup came as standard issue to the queues of starving Africans, a diet not conducive to all tastes, especially the Fingos. Mr Algie noting how 'Stadt natives jibbed at eating horse soup claiming it caused swollen heads and limbs that resulted in death'[58]. Critics have attacked Baden-Powell for providing such unsavoury and unsuitable rations to the African population. In fact, by the end of February, Baden-Powell, no doubt aware (as Hamilton confirms) that Europeans were also by now being forced to eat this 'damned and disagreeable dish'[59], gave orders for nothing to be issued in lieu ensuring that the 'Africans would be glad to eat it soon'[60].

On 8th February Baden-Powell received a "bombshell" telegram from Kitchener that forced him to undertake even more drastic measures. In a paragraph he was ordered to 'make supplies last four months' and 'to send as many women, children and natives as possible away should opportunity offer'[61]. It was a terrible blow as Baden-Powell's meticulous rationing plans had anticipated the arrival of relief forces over a much shorter time span. He now proposed 'to try to get all natives and foreign natives to leave this place by laying down stocks [of food] through Colonel Plumer at Kanya and stopping the sale in town'[62]. It was a controversial decision that has been lambasted by recent critics such as Thomas Pakenham as a ruthless policy of "leave or starve"[63]. For Baden-Powell it was clearly a decision based on extreme military imperatives. In fact, he took the trouble to inform and justify his policy to the local Baralong elite telling them 'that we were to hang on for four months and that though the food would suffice for whites and Baralongs, it would not be enough for the other outside natives as well'—the latter 'must therefore be told to escape as soon as possible and make their way to Kanya'[64]. It represented a terrible dilemma but, in its defence, Baden-Powell was already acutely aware of starvation deaths in the stadt (by 23rd February he himself had recorded at least three dead). Moreover, during February, there had been successful breakouts by various groups of escapees which may have given him confidence to try out this policy. For instance, on 22nd February 30 Africans had 'got away after dark towards Kanya' and on the 25th, 'about half' of 60 natives got through Boer lines[65]. Thirdly, in rationalizing his policy of enforced exodus (finally decided on 27th February), Baden-Powell not only provided rations and an armed escort for the departing Africans, but also, perhaps (rather naïvely), reached an agreement with the local Boer authorities to allow safe passage. A sympathetic Plaatje thus recorded the preparations made for departure with the arrival of a 'waggon-load of mule flesh' delivered as rations for the journey out. His account confirmed the extreme state of starvation then existing amongst the "foreign" or Transvaal African groups:

'I saw horse flesh for the first time being treated as human food stuff ... it looked like meat with nothing unusual about it but when they went to the slaughter pole for the third time and found there was no meat left and brought the heads and feet, I was moved to see the long ears and bald heads... the recipients, however, were all very pleased to get these heads and they ate them nearly raw'[66].

In the event the evacuation proved to be a disastrous failure from the start as the full escort failed to turn up and the Boers opened fire. Plaatje records the resultant tragic scenes:

'When a start was made from the river there arose cries of "Mma, Mma" (sic), children starting after their mothers and women after their children in the dark; but, after passing the BSA camp besides the heavy treads of twice 900 feet, there reigned a dead silence ... the volunteers failed to turn up and 12 men being unable to very well fight and drive 900 people at the same time the Boers scattered the whole crowd in every direction'[67].

As Baden-Powell confirmed, the 'two or three shots' fired by Boer snipers had caused 'widespread panic' and a subsequent second attempt, after Baden-Powell had re-negotiated a truce, ended in failure as the Boers reneged on their guarantee, 'to the effect that they would let native women and children go away—provided they went by day'[68]. This second *daytime* exodus near Game Tree was thus decimated as the Boers 'opened a fearful fire' amounting, in the view of Ross to, 'nothing else but cold-blooded murder'[69]. A deeply chastened Baden-Powell and the shocked garrison authorities were thus forced to send out doctors 'to render what assistance they could'[70].

It was a tragic end to this particular phase of the Siege, this disaster at the end of February being matched by the growing evidence of disease (a potential dysentery and typhoid epidemic) as well as widespread malnutrition amongst the children of the garrison. This included recorded outbreaks of "Brandsick"[71] or scabs. For the beleaguered garrison, however, much worse was to follow during the remaining three months of the Siege.

1   Algie *Diary*, 1 Jan 1900.
2   Ross *Diary*, 3 Jan 1900.
3   Craufurd, *A Nurse's Diary*. Such shelling caused anger and outrage across the garrison, Ross calling for 'retribution, sharp and severe', Ross *Diary*, 1 Jan 1900.
4   Ross *Diary*, 20 Jan 1900.
5   *Ibid*, 24 Jan. See also Algie *Diary*, 24 Jan.
6   Plaatje, 2 Jan 1900, *Mafeking Diary*, p 76.
7   Ross *Diary*, 1 Feb 1900.
8   Algie *Diary*, 10 Feb 1900. See also Chapter 2.
9   Ross *Diary*, 10 Jan 1900.
10  Ross *Diary*, 15 Jan 1900.
11  Baillie, 19 Jan 1900, *Siege*, p. 122.
12  *ibid*. See also Ross *Diary*, 3 Jan 1900.
13  Baillie, 1 Feb 1900, *Siege*, p. 122.
14  *ibid*, 30 Jan 1900, p 118. The second Boer sniper killed was almost certainly the same "veteran" observed by Ross on 15 Jan. See Endnote 10.
15  Ross *Diary*, 9 Jan 1900.
16  B-Powell, 4 Jan 1900, Staff Diary, B.P.P.
17  B-Powell, 12 and 18 Feb, Staff Diary, B.P.P.
18  Plaatje, *Mafeking Diary*, pp 105–6.
19  *ibid*. 6 Jan 1900, p 79.
20  *ibid*. 6 Jan 1900, p 82.
21  B-Powell, 3 Jan 1900, Staff Diary, B.P.P.
22  Plaatje, *Mafeking Diary*, 5 Jan 1900, p 80.
23  B-Powell, 7 Jan 1900, Staff Diary, B.P.P.
24  *ibid*, 6 Jan 1900.
25  Ross *Diary*, 27 Jan 1900.
26  *ibid*, 28 Jan 1900.
27  Baillie, 25 Jan, *Siege*, p 110.
28  Ross *Diary*, 1 Feb 1900.
29  B-Powell, 25 Feb 1900, Staff Diary, B.P.P.
30  Plaatje, 5 Feb, *Mafeking Diary*, p 80.
31  Hamilton, *Siege of Mafeking*, p 196.
32  *ibid*, pp 197-8.
33  Algie *Diary*, 23 Jan 1900.

# The ordeal escalates—January to February 1900 113

34  B-Powell, 21 and 22 Jan 1900, Staff Diary B.P.P.
35  B-Powell, Indaba Lekoko and Council, 22 Jan 1990 *ibid.*
36  Ross *Diary*, 11 Jan 1900.
37  *ibid.*
38  B-Powell, 7 Jan 1900, Staff Diary B.P.P.
39  Ross *Diary*, 29 Jan 1900.
40  Hamilton, *Siege of Mafeking*, p 200.
41  Ross *Diary*, 17 Jan 1900.
42  B-Powell, 1 and 15 Jan 1900, Staff Diary, B.P.P.
43  Hamilton, *Siege of Mafeking*, p 200.
44  Algie *Diary*, 21 Jan 1900.
45  *ibid*, 11 Feb 1900.
46  Wilson, *S African Memories*, p 202.
47  Baillie, 31 Jan 1900, *Siege*, p 119.
48  Ross *Diary*, 20 Jan 1900.
49  *ibid* 19 Jan 1900.
50  Wilson, *S African Memories*, pp 183-4.
51  Ross *Diary*, 31 Jan 1900.
52  Plaatje, 3 Jan 1900, *Siege of Mafeking*, p 76.
53  Ross *Diary*, 9 Feb 1900.
54  *ibid*, 6 Feb 1900.
55  Plaatje, 6 Feb 1900, *Siege of Mafeking*, p 93.
56  Baillie, 10 Feb, *Siege*, p 133. See also, the comments of Ada Cock, who on 27 Feb, observed the African children 'that come here begging for food. Their legs are like sticks and their knees like the knob and one has nothing to give them'. Midgley, *Petticoat in Mafeking*, p 68.
57  Algie *Diary*, 19 Feb 1900.
58  *ibid*, 27 Feb 1900.
59  Hamilton, *Siege of Mafeking*, p 226.
60  B-Powell, 27 Feb1900, Staff Diary, B.P.P.
61  Mafeking Day Book (CSO) Kitchener to B-Powell, 21 Jan 1900 (read Mafeking 8 Feb) in T. Jeal, *Baden Powell*, (London 1989) p 265 and 619.
62  B-Powell, 8 Feb 1900, Staff Diary.
63  See Pakenham, *The Boer War*, pp 407-9.
64  B-Powell, 10 Feb 1900, Staff Diary, B.P.P.
65  *ibid*, 22 and 25 Feb 1900, Staff Diary, B.P.P.
66  Plaatje, 27 Feb,900, *Mafeking Diary*, p 108.
67  *ibid*, p 109.
68  B-Powell, 27 and 28 Feb, Staff Diary, B.P.P.
69  Ross *Diary*, 1 March 1900.
70  *ibid.*
71  Cock, 14 Feb 1900, Midgley, *Petticoat in Mafeking*, p 66.

# The final desperate weeks—March to April 1900

*The garrison is famished, that is, in reality, the kernel of our situation. Our energies are exhausted because our vital processes are insufficiently nurtured. We are all listless; we feel that the siege has been a strain of the most severe description and we are holding ourselves in for the final rally...determined to hold the town and occupy, till the end, our posts.*

Hamilton, *Siege of Mafeking*
30th April 1900

January and February had been an extremely traumatic time for the hard-pressed inhabitants of Mafeking but, in many respects, the following two months would emerge as the critical period of the siege. As the Boers sustained a relentless military pressure (Mr Algie recording one barrage by Old Creechy of 34 shells on Saturday 3rd March[1]), the garrison produced more innovations to confound the enemy. The most significant of these was the invention of "dynamite bombs", a crude form of grenade ostensibly invented by Lieutenant Feltham of the Protectorate Regiment and 'made from jam tins and...very handy for throwing'. On Sunday 4th March these crude rather eccentric devices scored a notable military success in the Brickfields as Feltham, deploying these grenades both by hand and even by fishing rod! proved 'instrumental in ensuring the success of Captain FitzClarence and Captain Williams's reoccupation of a trench in the Brickfields'[2]. The new home built garrison gun, the "Wolf" was also tried out on the east trench firing about seven shells at 1,000 yards at the Boers. However, by the end of March the somewhat overused breech had blown out. According to Ross the following, (in hindsight, rather amusing), conversation took place:

| | |
|---|---|
| **BP** (On the telephone) to Panzera at the Brickfields: | Can the Wolf reach their big gun? |
| **Panzera:** | I think so, by putting in an extra charge of powder, but I am afraid the breech will not stand it. |
| **BP:** | Try |
| **Panzera** (later): | Have fired the gun and the breech has burst. |
| **BP:** | Damn![3] |

The Boers responded by deploying new home-made shrapnel shells, which caused increasing casualties amongst both people and livestock within the garrison precincts. Another new military innovation deployed by the Boer attackers was wire-operated 250 lb nitro-glycerine and dynamite mines which were left behind in vacated trenches in a vain bid to catch the garrison defenders unaware. Fortunately most of these were successfully defused[4]. On the British side, by early March most of the extensive trench network had been completed, trenches often acquiring variations of London street names, eg Regent's Circus, Oxford Street, etc, while the main Boer trench on the Brickfields 40 yards away was appropriately nicknamed, 'Hounds Ditch'.

During the two main Brickfields attacks launched during this period fighting could be ferocious and the often hand-to-hand encounters produced numerous examples of both black and white valour including "coloured" Sergeant-Major Taylor injured and fatally wounded by two successive shell bursts. At times, however, the fighting degenerated into farce with, for instance, the rival British and Boer sides in the Brickfield trenches 'throwing stones at each other', an incident repeated on the 10<sup>th</sup> March when both sides also discarded their rifles[5]! Truces, increasingly rare and usually held on Sundays, preserved the remnants of a "gentlemen's war" with friendly exchanges of newspapers and rations, but even these were often violated if either side were seen to be making war-like preparations on this ostensibly "holy day".

On the "home front" behind the garrison defences there was an increasingly rapid deterioration in the standard of life for most citizens. Rationing tightened considerably and, by early April, Orders had reduced bread rations from eight to six ounces with increasing restrictions on the sale of green mealies and cattle. Bread, a staple part of the garrison diet, had now become a luxury item. For European and African alike, the crude substitute (designed to replace the lost two ounces of bread ration) was a bitter porridge made from oats called "sowen". Made by soaking forage oats in water for a long time, skimming off the husks and scum (which could be used for feeding fowls) and then boiling up the remainder with added salt it was, perhaps, appropriately described by Baden-Powell as 'like paste used for bill-boards'[6].

During these two critical months, however, both European and African sources again highlight the valuable and increasingly critical role played by the indigenous armed black contingents. Just as the Game Tree battle of December 1899 had produced many white heroes so the great cattle raids and forays into Boer lines of March and April 1900 produced a significant crop of black heroes. Most singled out for praise were the Baralong cattle raiders. On 3<sup>rd</sup> March, for instance, Ross recalled a great deception of the enemy with two Baralongs who 'engaged themselves as servants to the Boers craftily returning at night

## The final desperate weeks—March to April 1900

with 43 fine head of Boer oxen'[7]. At times the Baralong raiding parties successfully engaged their hated Boer enemies in open battle. Most notable of these skirmishes was the Madibi ambush of 13th March when an 18-strong Baralong raiding party, led by the much-fêted Sergeant Abrahams, who, observing Boers following on their spoor, had doubled back on their own trail and ambushed them at short range. A most impressed Ross recorded their report, a rare first-hand and colourful African account of one of the most successful actions of the Siege and one which revealed the full extent of guile, resourcefulness and sheer raw courage of Baden-Powell's black auxiliaries.

> 'Twenty five of us went out... when we got to Madibi about 14 miles out we found the Boers were following our spoor so we hid on top of a kopje. The Boers saw us from the flat and fired at us at long range. When they came a little closer we fired and we saw we had hit one of the men who had stripes on his arm. The Boers went away ... so we left this place and went down to the railway lines at Madibi and got into the gravel pits (formerly used as ballast holes). By and by the Boers again came up following our spoor ... we waited until they came up quite close and then fired a volley at them killing eight and wounding seven and killing three or four of their horses. We brought in the arms and horses of the two we killed... others are dead but we could not get their things as the Boers took them away. After our volley the Boers galloped away'[8].

For the Mafeking African community this was seen as a great victory over their hated Boer oppressors. Plaatje testified to the ferocity of this brutal clash of arms between the two antagonistic foes in which no quarter was given, one Baralong 'hitting him [a Boer]' on the ground and he 'wounding one of our chaps on the buttocks before another hit him on the forehead'. It was 'a brief but very hot battle'. Plaatje gleefully recorded the booty which included horses ('a beautiful grey gelding') and 'two rifles... a splendid pair of Martinis made especially for the ZAR by Wesley Richards' and 'stamped very neatly "J J Jonck, ZAR 1900" with a circle'[9]. African casualties amounted to only two wounded (one slightly) their Boer enemy suffering eight dead.

These successes had a massive catalytic effect as the Baralong raiders rapidly expanded their activities. A "white man's war" was rapidly becoming a mixed race war. Plaatje reported on 19th March, for instance, that up to 1,000 armed Baralongs were now 'scattered all over the country. Two hundred of them are at Madibi and they have two Maxims. Mathakgong's name [a notorious raider] is a household name on every farm... they say he has killed many Boers at their farms during the last month, including women and children'[10]. Such successes clearly dismayed the Boer besiegers especially as they had such major implications for the post-war social order. News of such white reverses at the hands of armed blacks probably also accounts for the increasing frequency and frantic nature of the protests and even threats communicated from Snyman, the local Boer commander, to Baden-Powell. Snyman (like Cronje before him) continued to stress the extreme dangers of deploying armed blacks. Baden-Powell's repeated angry rejections of the protest did not just reflect his awareness of the hypocrisy of the Boer case (the Boers continued to deploy armed cattle guards around Mafeking defence lines). As long as such raids were crucial to the survival of the garrison Baden-Powell was clearly now prepared to bypass the normal imperatives of social order. As Major Baillie succinctly confirmed: 'This success has naturally much pleased the natives and encouraged them greatly for future raids, which is most useful as the results feed us and harass the Boers'[11]. Other African and coloured groups also distinguished themselves. Mr Algie noted in his diary one day: 'The Fingos came back from their looting expedition with five head of cattle,' the Baralongs this time 'not so successful—they were only able to capture one donkey'[12]. This is not to say that the Boers did not have their own successes. In early April, owing to a Boer ambush only four returned alive out of a 30 strong Fingo "looting expedition"[13].

## The final desperate weeks—March to April 1900

In the front line trenches even more spectacular successes were scored by the European-led black contingent "Mackenzie's boys", whose one night raid on Jackal Tree resulted in the death of 'one Boer and an African' and the capture of three horses and rifles[14]. Of all the coloured and African contingents the much admired Cape Boys, known for their precision shooting and outstanding loyalty (they constituted most of the garrison execution squads!), were, perhaps, the most daring. They engaged in frequent verbal confrontations with their Boer protagonists accompanied often by racial taunts. One incident involved the staging of a mock entertainment in which the Cape Boys danced and called on the Boers to send them some of their ladies. This 'so chafed the Boers' that 'one of them, either attracted by the music or bursting with repartee, popped up his head and was incontinently shot by a wily Cape Boy'. The admiring but somewhat shocked Major Baillie commented, 'They have a distinct sense of humour, though possibly a somewhat grim one'[15].

If there were black heroes there were also black victims. By the end of March it was clear that the food situation for significant numbers of Africans trapped within the garrison perimeter was becoming critical. By early March deaths from starvation had become commonplace. On the 12th Algie reported how one European (Wenham) had found 'two natives who had died from starvation'[16]. Government soup kitchens expanded rapidly, Plaatje noting the afternoon queues of 'hundreds of natives'[17] at the nearby Government kitchen. In March, Ross also observed how 'the lower class of natives' was 'beginning to suffer the pangs of starvation very severely; one poor devil was found on the south outskirts of the town this afternoon terribly emaciated and had to be carried to the hospital where they gave him a good feed'[18]. A significant and distressing sign of large-scale starvation was the recourse to the consumption of stray dogs as well as horsemeat. Mr Ross recorded sympathetically, if a little patronizingly, one heart-rending scene that he witnessed after the weekly cull (by shooting) of stray dogs by the Town Ranger:

'The natives congregate in crowds as soon as one poor dog is shot... it resembles a children's school treat when sweets are thrown; they make a frantic rush and almost tear the carcass to pieces in their haste to obtain possession. The next moment it is in their cooking pots and eaten half raw'[19].

There were other desperate attempts by starving Africans to supplement the mainly horsemeat and sowen diet. On 15th March for instance it was tersely reported how two men, Grayson and Stewart, on a journey through the stadt found 'starving natives eating the following: "crabs" [fresh water crayfish]; ox hide; dead dog'[20].

As more soup kitchens were opened to cope with the increasing crisis, there was some contemporary if, as we shall see, misplaced criticism. Hamilton, for instance, deplored the charging of three pence for each bowl of soup[21]. Neilly painted a particularly desperate situation, observing:

'I saw them fall down on the veldt and lie where they had fallen too weak to go on their way. The sufferers...who were mostly little boys.... Hunger had them in its grip and many of them were black spectres and living skeletons... their ribs literally breaking their shrivelled skin—men, women and children. Probably hundreds died from starvation or disease that always accompanies famine. Certain it is that many were found dead on the velt'[22].

A closer examination of the sources, however, reveals that, as Tim Jeal[23] has already indicated, starvation amongst the black population was by no means universal and the authorities were not wholly inactive as both contemporary and more recent critics such as Brian Gardner[24] and Thomas Pakenham[25] have suggested. The heaviest mortality rate, by far, was in fact almost certainly experienced by the largely homeless Transvaal "Uitlander group", encompassing the Zambesians and Shangaanis. Mr Algie states emphatically that 'the starving natives were principally Shangaans'[26]. When Plaatje witnessed another similar dog culling scene on 15th March it was highly significant that it was 'our local Zambesian friends' who 'unearth them immediately the ranger's assistants left the scene, and promptly cooked them for dinner, which gave the Baralong sections of the community the impression that there is more in a dog than they were ever told there was'[27]. Even Neilly confirms after his "holocaust" description that 'the Baralongs proper were not so badly off; the least fortunate were the strange natives who came in from the Transvaal as refugees when the war started and the slaves and servants of the Baralong nation'[28].

This last phrase also helps explain why this effectively isolated group also suffered disproportionately. It is clear from many sources that little aid or support was provided for them by the permanent black residents. Indeed, Baillie noted the high degree of antipathy existing between the established Baralong community and these itinerant groups. 'The Shangaans...' he noted, 'were detested by the other natives and consequently it is very hard to look after them properly... so much so that on Mr Vere ordering his Basuto servant to make some soup for a starving Shangaan he had picked up, the Basuto indignantly protested'[29]. Plaatje similarly noted how the majority of the soup kitchen refugees were 'made-up of the blackish races of this continent—mostly Zulus and Zambesians', who, 'venerate the Civil Commissioner and call me "ngwana molimo" [young god]'. He continued; 'It is really pitiful to see one who was too unfortunate to hear soon enough that there was a residency in Mafeking, and, being too weak to work, never had a chance to steal anything during the last six days, and so had nothing to eat... it was a miserable scene to be surrounded by about 50 hungry beings, agitating the engagement of your pity and to see one of them succumb to his agonies and fall backwards with a dead thud'[30]. Final confirmation that *mass* starvation was confined to the minority "Transvaal African" groups was provided by a, perhaps, more impartial observer, Lady Sarah

Wilson. She supplied further damning evidence on black divisions confirming again 'the Johannesburg tribes' who 'were the ones to suffer most from hunger in spite of Government relief and the fact that they had plenty of money for they had done most of the trench work and had been well paid'. She continued; 'the reason was that they were strangers to the other natives who had their own gardens to supplement their food allowance...blacks are strangely unkind and hard to each other and remain quite unmoved if a [to them] unknown man dies of starvation although he be of their own colour'[31].

Moreover, it is also possible that these Transvaal African victims numbered significantly fewer than has been hitherto suggested. Algie noted on 16th March that 'since the 27th February exodus approximately 1,000 had left town for the North'[32]. Similarly on 17th March, Plaatje confided that there were in fact 'very few Shangaanis and Zambesians and the majority had left this place and gone up country'[33]. On 22nd March a thorough census of the stadt by Plaatje and his white colleagues revealed 'no fewer than 5,448 people in the stadt out of 10,000 at the commencement of hostilities... as quite half the population have been clearing out in fours and fives as the tension became more and more strained'[34].

For the Baralong themselves while food was undoubtedly in short supply most survived and a few even prospered in the artificial market conditions created by the Siege. As Lady Wilson observed many Baralongs cultivated extensive vegetable gardens from which even the European towns people were supplied (albeit at rising costs) giving 'an impression of prosperity'[35]. On occasion fresh produce could even be obtained from outside the garrison defences. Plaatje noted on 9th March how some African women 'went out in the direction of Signal Hill to gather green makotone etc from their fields', a touching scene in which racial animosity was unusually absent as 'young Boers... told them to glean in haste and return before their parents came as they would not permit them to take away any'[36]. Later, on 13th March, Plaatje noted the often less stringent Boer cordons as

## The final desperate weeks—March to April 1900

'women are now always going out to Moleloane [a village five miles north-west of Mafeking] and coming home with lots of melons and kaffir corn... we are wondering why the Boers permit them to go out as, for a while, they had not previously even been allowing them to get some bushes for fuel behind the Convent on Sundays'[37].

For the Baralongs in particular an even richer source of income came from shares in the proceeds of the many cattle raids. Mr Algie noted the 'generous scale of rewards allocated by the Colonel after one successful cattle raid by Mathlagong and 40 natives. This included £1 to £14 per head for 'recovering strange animals under fire' and for enemy's stock brought in one quarter belonged to the Government the remainder to be purchased by the Government at full price'[38]. Within the stadt itself, often-illegal horse-trading and cattle trading was widely prevalent with significant cash sums exchanged. On occasions even Government interference was defied. When the Colonel reprimanded the normally compliant Lekoko for, 'slaughtering some plundered cattle' without giving the commissariat the chance of buying them, Lekoko's reply was, 'No *Cooler*... we have been giving you a fourth of all the loot and you said you did not care for it'[39]. Other Baralong who owned fowls became heavily engaged in a thriving egg trade, eggs fetching sixpence each[40]. Indeed the amount of cash specie retained in African hands was cited by Baden-Powell and others as the main reason for the resort to the issue of siege paper currency earlier in March of that year[41].

There were other ingenious strategies for survival. Several Africans took advantage of the thriving trade in shell cases eagerly purchased by the Europeans as souvenirs. Ada Cock recalled how a Big Ben shell which 'came over the base and stuck in the mud was picked up by a "Kaffir" and 'sold.. for £6'[42]. On rare occasions "mother nature" provided a welcome helping hand. In late March a massive swarm of locusts provided a major supplement to African diets, Mr Algie (and others) noting that 'because of the locust swarm there were not so many natives at the soup kitchens'[43].

For the much-valued African political and military elites life was much more bearable—by Government Notice 192 for instance 'natives bearing arms were given regular rations, including one quart of sowen daily'⁴⁴. Educated Africans such as court interpreter Plaatje survived on often quite generous weekly Government rations that included groceries (tea, coffee, sugar, pepper and salt) vegetables (green mealies, beet, cabbage, turnips and carrots etc from the gardens and fields on the riverbeds) and preserved meat⁴⁵.

A good indicator of the growing distress amongst some, especially the minority alien African groups was the rising crime rate. Theft became a key strategy of survival and, from early March onwards, the crime rate within Mafeking soared. Many of these perpetrators of thefts, especially in the gardens of the stadt and the European residential areas were again significantly Shangaans. Thus, a nervous Ada Cock noted with alarm both their culpability and the close links with the ongoing food crisis, which escalated into possibly wild rumours of active cannibalism.

> 'There were a lot of Shangaans under the trees here and they had been stealing my fowls. I have only nine left. They are dying of starvation. I don't know what they had been living on the but smell is something dreadful. They had been moved up to the empty Police Barracks and are killing and eating all the dogs they can get. Arthur [the caretaker] says he believes they ate their dead chum who was never carted away... someone said he smelt human flesh roasting. It is quite dangerous to let children run about by themselves. I don't know⁴⁶'.

Hamilton also remarked on the growing phenomena of domestic animal thefts with 'natives... at their wits end' having 'resorted to a variety of dishes which under more favourable circumstances they would not touch. Pet dogs which are sleek, family cats that are fat, are stolen nightly from the hotels and empty houses... they are invariably traced to native marauders

## The final desperate weeks—March to April 1900

who, inspired by hunger, prowl around by night seeking what they might devour'[47].

The rising crime rate was reflected in Plaatje's own court records in which theft of fuel and food cases predominated, (four out of seven listed on 20th March court sitting). The defendants were invariably "foreign natives". The cases arraigned included an old Zulu 'charged with stealing wood' and significantly an 'old miserable half-starved Shangaan charged with theft of green mealies' notably 'the property of the Chief Lekoko'. The latter's plea was 'guilty under provocation—hunger'. On the 29th yet another Shangaan was charged with the theft of a horse; his plea was 'guilty under provocation', as he had been living on 'thepe' (a vegetable)[48]. "Foreign natives" caught stealing in the stadt gardens could receive rough justice. 'One heathen' caught 'stealing garden produce' was 'nearly beaten to death' by a Baralong mob yet another testament to the growing inter-African friction[49].

The penalties for theft became progressively harsher and by early April repeated theft had become a capital offence. On 2nd April, for instance, 'a native' twice found guilty of theft was executed at sundown, again by a firing party of six Cape Boys[50]. Others received heavy floggings for first offences. Social control was also tightened. Already from 8th February onwards (significantly as the food crisis escalated) 'no natives were allowed in town without a pass'. Three "classes" of Africans were established—permanent town employees, permanent employees outside town and stadt folk. Each received coloured tickets in the same manner as in Kimberley and this may have helped control the crime rate as pass violators could be brought before the courts[51].

These two desperate months constituted perhaps the most controversial period in Baden-Powell's career. Critics have accused him not only of discriminatory rationing practices but also of deliberate neglect of emergency food supplies for the African population. However, these can again be seriously contended. Although "BP" as[52] Jeal pointed out, was by no means even-handed in his food distribution with superior rations allocated to both black elite groups and Europeans as a whole, even Jeal the most vociferous contemporary critic concedes that, as early as March, when the Colonel 'got to know of the state of affairs he instituted soup kitchens... where horses were boiled in huge caldrons and the savoury mess doled out in pints and quarts to all comers'[53]. Significantly, 'some of the people—those employed on the works—paid for food; the remainder who were in the majority obtained it free'[54]. On 20th March, Algie recorded an increasingly rapid response to the African food crisis with 'the distribution of food... reorganized and everyone had something to eat[55]. Indeed, [by direct order of Baden-Powell] about 30 half–starved Shangaans were put into the Cape Police stables and looked after there'[56]. Moreover, it is possible that some of the earlier recorded harsher measures such as excessive charging for soup were unofficially adopted by junior officers or administrators attached to the kitchens and without the knowledge of the ever-busy Baden-Powell. Hence the comment of Colonel Hore, one of the more humanitarian presiding judges who expressed sympathy towards many theft defendants, and specifically blamed the 'soup kitchen people' for those 'shameful deeds... they don't feed the people at all'. In the event by mid – late April as Ross, himself often critical of Baden-Powell, confirmed 'BP has done everything he could to alleviate distress among the natives none of whom need now starve... if they are not too lazy to walk as far as the horse meat soup kitchens'[57].

The total number of deaths from starvation amongst the African population will never be accurately known. A terribly tragedy did occur but, in the event, the overall mortality rate as Plaatje's census figures would suggest, can be counted in the few hundreds rather than thousands. Moreover, any situation approaching mass starvation only occurred amongst the trapped and relatively isolated Transvaal African groups, particularly the Shangaanis of whom it would seem only about 500 remained within the town precincts by the end of March[58]. After the obvious mistake of enforced exodus of these groups in late February and the subsequent disastrous failure, it can be argued that Baden-Powell did make strenuous efforts to alleviate the deteriorating conditions of those left behind. Indeed, Plaatje, the sole recorded African voice from the Siege laid no blame at the door of Baden-Powell; his finger of guilt pointed solely at the 'abominable Transvaal Boers'[59] who had driven these unfortunate people into the Mafeking compounds at the start of the Siege. Indeed, in a public letter published in the *Mafeking Mail* at the end of March, Baden-Powell himself resolutely defended his rationing policies to both his European and African critics such as Lekoko. Contrasting his admittedly relatively harsh regime with the far worst prospects of Boer captivity he wrote:

'As regards the smallness of our rations we could of course live well on full rations for a week or two and then give in to the "women slaughterers" and let them take their vengeance on the town whereas by limiting our amount of daily food we can make certain of outlasting all their efforts against us. The present ration, properly utilized, is a fairly full one as compared with those issued in other sieges'[60].

While aspects of Baden-Powell's "social policies" during the Siege will no doubt remain controversial, in other spheres he proved himself an exceptional political and military leader. Even at the most pressurized times of these critical months of 1900 European and African morale continued to be sustained by his ingenious and original morale building exercises. Sunday concerts and entertainments were conducted even in the midst of enemy bombardment. On Sunday 5th April, for instance, the garrison was treated to a volunteer sports display by the Bechuanaland Rifles and a fancy dress competition[61]! Moreover, contrary to the claims of his critics Baden-Powell did often praise and reward the individual exploits of his African as well as his white defenders. On 11th April, for instance, from his famous "lookout position" BP observed 'a very plucky bit of native work when an exceptionally brave African herd boy, under deliberately targeted Boer shell fire (combined nine-pounder and one-pounder Maxim fire), successfully rounded up and rescued a large section of the garrison's herd of horses. The Colonel promptly rewarded the boy with a £5 note[62]. Again when 20 of Abraham's Boys successfully defeated a 150 strong massed Boer attack on the Brickfields trenches 'letting them have two or three volleys' and 'bowling over four or five of the enemy' Baden-Powell mentioned all of them in General Orders that very same evening[63]. White as well as black youths also performed sterling tasks. As mentioned earlier the Cadet Corps supervised by Lord Edward Cecil, and made up of white boys over the age of nine but too young for full military service, acted, often under heavy shell fire as messengers, postmen and orderlies providing inspiration, as we know for Baden-Powell's later establishment of the Boy Scout Movement.

Above all, regardless of his critics there is little doubt that Baden-Powell's personal qualities and his indomitable spirit, provided the ultimate source of inspiration for the defenders of Mafeking. Angus Hamilton has provided a rare but vivid appreciation of Baden-Powell at the height of his powers, one which, while exposing his undoubted egotism, also reveals his special mesmeric qualities including his stoicism and his unrelenting sense of duty that made him such an effective *military* leader.

> 'Colonel Baden-Powell is young, as men go in the Army, with a keen appreciation of the possibilities of his career, swayed by ambition, indifferent to sentimental emotion. In stature he is short, while his features are sharp and smooth. He is eminently a man of determination, of great physical endurance and capacity, and of extraordinary reticence. His reserve is unbending... he does not go about freely since he is tied to his office through the multitudinous cares of his command and he is chiefly happy when he can snatch

the time to escape on one of those nocturnal, silent expeditions, which alone calm and assuage the perpetual excitement of his present existence. Outwardly, he maintains an impenetrable screen of self-control, observing with a cynical smile the foibles and caprices of those around him. He seems ever bracing himself to be on guard against a moment in which he should be swept by some unnatural and spontaneous enthusiasm, in which by a word, by an expression of face, by a movement, or in the turn of a phrase, he should betray the rigours of the self control under which he lives. Every passing townsman regards him with curiosity not unmixed with awe. Every servant in the hotel watches him, and he, as a consequence, seldom speaks without a preternatural deliberation and an air of decisive finality. He seems to close every argument with a snap, as though the steel manacles of his ambition had checkmated the emotions of the man in the instincts of the officer. He weighs each remark before he utters it, suggests by his manner, as by his words, that he has considered the different effects it might conceivably have on any mind at the expression of his own mind. As an officer, he has given to Mafeking a complete and assured security, to the construction of which he has brought a very practical knowledge of the conditions of Boer warfare, of the Boers themselves and of the strategic worth of the adjacent areas. His espionagic excursions to the Boer lines have gained him an intimate and accurate knowledge of the value of the opposing forces and a mass of data by which he can immediately counteract the enemy's attack. He loves the night, and after his return from the hollows in the veldt, where he has kept many anxious vigils, he lies awake hour after hour upon his camp mattress in the veranda, tracing out in his mind, the various means and agencies by which he can forestall their move, which unknown to them, he had personally watched. ... As he makes his way across our lines the watchful sentry strains his eyes a little more to keep the figure of the Colonel before him, until the undulations of the veldt conceal his progress. ... He goes on never faltering, bending for a moment behind a clump of rocks, screening himself next behind some bushes, crawling upon his hands and knees, until his movements, stirring a few loose stones, create a thin grating noise in the vast silence about him. His head is low, his eyes gaze straight upon the camp of the enemy; in a little he moves again, his inspection is over, and he either changes to a fresh point or startles some dozing sentry as he slips back into town'[64].

There was however one "spectre of death", disease which was beyond even Baden-Powell's considerable powers to control. As mentioned earlier in February, outbreaks of diphtheria and dysentery had been reported and, by the 10th March, Algie had reported 'typhoid amidst the whites with smallpox and scurvy amongst the natives'[65]. The enforced confinement of the defenders and the extreme state of malnutrition had ensured that by the end of March, 12½% of the garrison had been hospitalized owing to sickness, disease and casualties[66]. These figures do not include the many bedridden victims confined at home or those many unknown African victims in the stadt area. At the end of April Hamilton reported both its rapid spread and the devastating impact on garrison morale as "fever flags" floated over designated quarantine areas within the township.

'There are three such places; one is remote from our lines, well out into the veldt where it is not permitted to go, where... isolated and apart... is a family fighting against the ravages of diphtheria; between them and the stadt there is a smallpox reserve where a yellow jack droops from the trees behind whose shadows the tents of the patients have been pitched. Still nearer into town and nearer the hospital the flag of mercy protects that building in which there is much malaria, some typhoid and a few cases of enteric fever... It is in these quarters that we, who are hale and hearty, look with anxious eyes. There are many here that will pay with their lives as tributes to the Siege[67]. It was an excessively gloomy but fitting epitaph to over six and a half months of mounting ordeal for the defenders of Mafeking.

1   Algie *Diary*, 3 March 1900.
2   *Ibid*, 4 March 1900.
3   Ross *Diary*, 26 March 1900.
4   Baillie, 13 March 1900, *Siege*, p. 175.
5   Algie *Diary*, 9 & 10 March 1900.
6   Algie *Diary*, 29 March 1900.
7   Ross *Diary*, 3 March 1900.
8   *Ibid*, 14 March 1900.
9   Plaatje, *Mafeking Diary*, p. 117.
10  *ibid*, p. 122.
11  Baillie, 13 March 1900, *Siege*, p. 176.
12  Algie *Diary*, 23 March 1900.
13  *Ibid*, 8 April 1900.
14  Baillie, 17 March 1900, *Siege*, p. 178.
15  *ibid*, 8 April 1900.
16  Algie *Diary*, 12 March 1900.
17  Plaatje, *Mafeking Diary*, p. 118.
18  Ross *Diary*, 9 March 1900.
19  *ibid*, 25 March 1900.
20  Algie *Diary*, 15 March 1900.
21  Hamilton, *Siege of Mafeking*, p. 249.
22  Neilly, *Besieged with BP,* pp. 227–9.

23 Jeal, *Baden-Powell*, pp. 269–73. See especially his comments on Pakenham's alleged misinterpretation of Neilly's observations.
24 See B. Gardner, *Mafeking*, pp. 154-7
25 See Pakenham, *The Boer War*, pp. 405–409.
26 Algie *Diary*, 16 March 1900.
27 Plaatje, *Mafeking Diary*, p. 119.
28 Neilly, *Besieged*.
29 Baillie, 15 March, *Siege*, pp. 209–10.
30 Plaatje, *Mafeking Diary*, pp. 124–5.
31 S. Wilson, *South African Memories*, p.101.
32 Algie *Diary*, 16 March 1900.
33 Plaatje, *Mafeking Diary*, p. 120.
34 *ibid*, p. 125.
35 Wilson, *South African Memories*, p. 101.
36 Plaatje, *Mafeking Diary*, p. 114.
37 *ibid, p 116*.
38 Algie *Diary*, 5 April 1900.
39 Plaatje, *Mafeking Diary*, p 101.
40 Baillie, 7 Feb, *Siege*, p. 127.
41 B-Powell, 10 March 1900, Staff Diary, B.P.P.
42 A. Cock, *Petticoat in Mafeking*, p. 64. Other lucrative sources of employment included carrying blankets for European troops, for which African "blanket boys" received a sixpence and part of their rations—Plaatje, *Diary* p 83.
43 Algie *Diary*, 23 March 1900.
44 *ibid* 11 April 1900.
45 Plaatje, *Mafeking Diary*, pp. 126–7.
46 Cock, *Petticoat in Mafeking*.
47 Hamilton, *Siege of Mafeking*, p. 288.
48 Plaatje, *Mafeking Diary*, pp. 122–3.
49 *Ibid*, p. 105.
50 Ross *Diary*, 2 April 1900.
51 Plaatje, *Mafeking Diary*, p. 96.
52 Jeal, *Baden-Powell*, p. 264.
53 Neilly, *Besieged*, pp. 228–9.
54 *Ibid*. This corrected Hamilton's earlier criticism of compulsory food payments for *all* Africans.
55 Algie *Diary*, 20 March 1900.
56 *Ibid*. See also BP Staff Diary, 14 March 1900 recording the establishment of a Board 'to consider question of feeding the natives and suggesting any improvements'.
57 Ross *Diary*, 23 April 1900.

## The final desperate weeks—March to April 1900     133

58    This corresponds to Jeal's figures. Jeal, *Baden-Powell*, p. 272.
59    Plaatje, *Mafeking Diary*, p 125.
60    B-Powell, *Mafeking Mail*, 30 March 1900. Also reproduced in Plaatje, *ibid* pp. 131–3.
61    Algie *Diary*, 15 April 1900.
62    Ross *Diary*, 11 April 1900.
63    *Ibid*. See also BP Staff Diary, 14 April 1900 where Baden-Powell fulsomely praised and rewarded Baralong raiders at an *indaba* with Lekoko and his headmen.
64    Hamilton, *Siege of Mafeking*, pp.192–5.
65    Algie *Diary*, 10 March 1900.
66    Ross *Diary*, 30 March 1900.
67    Hamilton, *Siege of Mafeking*, p 287. Algie *Diary*, 16 March 1900.

# Chapter 10

## The relief of Mafeking— May 1900

Despite welcome news of the slow but steady progress of Colonel Plumer's relief force the garrison approached the transition from April to May with a palpable sense of foreboding. Ross reported: 'The enemy's main laager grows bigger every day and it is now known that Commandant Eloff is in charge of the enemy outside and so an extra keen watch is being kept. He has brought large reinforcements and we may soon expect a good deal of fighting'[1]. The 'dashing fellow' Sarel Eloff (1863 to 1924), renowned for his energy and aggression, had joined the Boer besiegers on 24th April, and as a Field-Cornet and nephew of President Kruger he enjoyed a position of high status and prestige amongst his Boer compatriots. Ada Cock disconsolately reinforced the mood of gloom: 'People seem to think the relief will come some time about the end of the month but I do not like to think about it'[2].

After its heaviest day of shelling on the 11th April, the feared Boer artillery piece, "Big Ben", was withdrawn, having fired 13,379 shells or '65 tons of cast iron'[3]. While some comfort was expressed at this there were other ominous signs of enhanced Boer determination if not an imminent offensive. On Sunday 6th May the already fragile concept of a "gentleman's war" evaporated as the Boers demonstrated a new unprecedented degree of ruthlessness by directly attacking a BSAP funeral. An outraged Ada Cock observed how 'the Boers were volleying at the funeral procession, the bullets falling about ten or 12 yards short. The funerals have always been at night but the Colonel thought he would have this one at seven in the morning and that is how the Boers behaved'[4]. A grim Ross confirmed that this despicable act had 'destroyed all future Sunday truces. No more sports etc for us. Very hard luck'[5]. By 9th May even "white flag communication" had been broken off. By then an outraged Baden-Powell had already promptly retaliated by ordering troops based at Fort Ayr and Fort Nelson to open continuous fire on the nearby Boer trenches[6]. Garrison morale was also hard-hit by news of the severe disablement of the black "hero" Sergeant Abrahams. He had been severely injured with Trooper Cook by an unexploded 94-pound shell, 'his left foot... blown in half from the heel to instep just hanging by the skin' with, as Ada Cock remembered, 'the hot blood running all over my hands'[7]. Nevertheless, his black military compatriots continued to achieve successes. Thus, Ross observed how 'Mackenzie's native boys managed to bowl over two of the enemy this morning on the railway lines and since then kept them from recovering the bodies. They had no Red Cross flag so our men were perfectly justified'[8]. There was, it would seem, a new ruthless edge to this prolonged war of attrition.

Such small skirmishes and individual human losses were matched by the depressing scenes of desolation throughout the town. Collateral damage after over seven months of Siege was now extensive. Scarcely a house was left undamaged. In early May, Ross vividly recorded the "Armageddon" atmosphere, in which parts of the town seemed to resemble a lunar landscape, and in which everyday life was conducted largely underground.

> 'Poor old Mafeking looks now a perfect hole of desolation; all the trees have been cut down for firewood, all the wooden fences torn up for a like purpose, the houses all in a

state of complete wreckage. There is not a single house or store in the town that has not at some time or another been severely punished by shellfire, many having to be pulled down as being dangerous; all the galvanized iron roofs of those standing are riddled with shrapnel and bullets, until they resembled enormous corrugated sieves. Black gaping holes here, there, and everywhere, showing where the shell passed through on its way to other damage or to kill, kill, kill. The shop windows that have not fallen in are nailed up by pieces of old iron, packing cases or anything else that could be used. Here and there can be seen a huge tarpaulin spread over a roof, endeavouring to keep the inmates at least dry. The ends of all the streets barricaded by large, heavy sheets of galvanized iron supported by large heavy buck-waggons and sandbags. Miniature loopholed forts made of sandbags dotted here and there about the town at different corners of streets. Protection holes dug out of the streets all over the town. Not a solitary unbroken window to be seen, not even the little curl of homely smoke to be seen coming out of the few chimneys that are left. Hardly a soul, man, woman, or child, to be seen about the streets, and the very few one does meet are white, hungry, gaunt-looking faces that make one shudder, and give one the blues. The whole town gives me the impression that this is what it will look like at the time the poor old Earth has had her last shaking up and the last Trumpet has been blown'[9].

The scale of destruction had already caused intense friction between Baden-Powell and elements of the civilian population. As early as March, a wearying Baden-Powell had received angry letters from the Mafeking Town Council imploring him 'to consider the question of damages and losses sustained by the whole of Mafeking as a result of the Siege', and demanding 'substantial compensation'[10]. By the end of March, he had, in typical blunt fashion, clamped down on this continual complaining. While reassuring them of imperial compensation he warned:

'Grousing is generally the outcome of funk on the part of the individual who grouses, and I hope that every right-minded man who hears any of it will shut it up with an appropriate remark or toe of his boot. Cavillers should keep quiet until the Siege is over and then they are welcome to write or talk until they are blue in the face... there are few individual grumblers—most of whom are known to me... it is these gentlemen that I desire to warn to keep quiet otherwise I shall have to take more stringent steps against them, but I should be ashamed if the fame of Mafeking and its heroic defence were to be marred by a whisper among envious outsiders, that there was any want of harmony or unity of purpose amongst us'[11].

By the start of May, Baden-Powell had far more serious military matters to concern him. A telegram from General Roberts (9th April) had again postponed the prospects for relief of the Siege from 8th May, to 10th June,[12] plunging Baden-Powell into another unexpected ration crisis. He was again forced to consider the unsavoury prospect of 'forcing natives away from Mafeking to save horse meat and save rations'[13]. In the same telegram, however, he demonstrated a degree of compassion and a determination to eventually compensate local Africans for any distress caused—'suggest in concluding peace to fine Boers cattle and repay looted loyalists and natives'[14]. A meeting held at the end of April with his key military confidants, Lord Cecil, Major Gould-Adams and Godley, revealed why Baden-Powell had again been forced into taking what might appear to have been unwarranted and extreme measures. By then the garrison's morale and fitness level had reached crisis point. The 'rush of sickness' combined with a cold snap and heavy rain had led to 'over 20 admissions to hospital in the previous 36 hours'[15]. Dysentery, malaria and typhoid were rife, with the prospect of a major epidemic. Baden-Powell knew that without fit and able-bodied defenders there was no prospect of survival for anyone in the garrison. The conclusions of this meeting were uncompromising. 'We all agreed the men reduced in strength by the continuance of low diet... small extras they normally purchased to supplement their diet were now failing... sickness is beginning to tell—fever and dysentery becoming prevalent and that not only can no reduction in rations be made but rather an increase is desirable'[16]. In his otherwise very sparse and generalized "memories" of the Siege, Major Godley distinctly remembers this crisis meeting 'with Gould-Adams and Cecil, at which we decided that a further reduction in rations was out of the question. At the same time we realized that to increase them from our small reserve stock would mean that all supplies would be finished by the end of May'. Furthermore, in a stark warning to Colonel Plumer, head of the relief force, Baden-Powell asserted, 'health of garrison can no longer go on to 10th June'[17].

Moreover, contrary to both his contemporary and current critics who accused him of perpetuating the Siege for his own self-glorification, Baden-Powell did actively consider, in the face of this major crisis 'withdrawing garrison, leaving civilians here'. Although this course of action would be 'undesirable in terms of loss or prestige, valuable property (including 18 locomotives)', he argued, that 'tactically' the British cause would 'not lose much as we could divert the enemy and even shut them up in Mafeking'[18]. On 2nd May Baden-Powell reiterated: 'if our relief founders after all I shall make an effort to withdraw the garrison'[19].

Furthermore, there was plenty of other ground-level evidence of a crisis by early May 1900. Horses for instance were 'now dying of poverty as fast as we can kill them for soup' and, on 10th May, Ross tersely recalled even more drastic measures being taken—'we have now commenced soup kitchens for whites. The stuff is horrible but we must live just a little bit longer'[20]. As Baden-Powell, no longer confident of a firm relief date, desperately held onto existing food stocks, further new "survival diets" were concocted, the most notorious being "brawn" a meal ostensibly invented by the Cape Boys from ox hides. Eventual ingredients included horse hooves, horse heads, cowhide, donkey meat, carpenters glue, spice and split peas'. Brawn was sold to Europeans at one shilling a pound, often to supplement sowen at sixpence a quart. As Ross wryly commented: 'One cannot get through much of this but the natives seem to appreciate it highly and get full up with it. I think everything in the place has been eaten except horseshoes and barbed wire'. Such was the scarcity that one 'artful Johnny' who had secreted a fowl in his dugout managed to sell it for 30 shillings![21]

Amongst the Mafeking African population, small pockets of starvation were still evident and were again illustrated by continually high crime levels. Both Baralongs and Europeans were forced to guard their cattle herds closely, the numbers of which however had remained relatively constant, largely owing to the continuing success of the garrison's African cattle raiders. On 28th April, Ada Cock recorded the dangers at night in the midst of an internal crime wave as 'the starving niggers are jumping cattle'[22]. By May 3rd she had resorted to desperate measures to protect her remaining cattle stocks after 'some natives stole granny's beautiful little cow...I let Willie [the caretaker] know at once and the Government sent detectives out. She was found yesterday half eaten. They have three boys in the trunk, two got away or rather they could not catch them. So now I have my revolver loaded and Willie has had chains made and put the chains around the waggon wheel and then padlocked it around their necks. The natives will have to kill them here if they want to now and then I will hear and give them a small pill!'[23]

For many others, notably the Baralong cattle raiding fraternity, opportunity was still rife. As Baden-Powell lamented, even the newly instituted Government sequestration operations to conserve food were being thwarted as, 'natives whose stock disappeared... had sent them away... to avoid having them commandeered'. The Colonel was forced to have 'all stock taken over by the ASC and put under our herds under Mr Whitfield[24].

In the midst of such trials and tribulations there were still occasional bouts of sardonic humour. Thus, one communication sent by Eloff to Baden-Powell the Boer commander, noting the garrison's regular Sunday habit of playing cricket matches, asked permission to bring a team into town one Sunday for a friendly game! This elicited the reply by Baden-Powell, a master of sardonic humour, that, although the garrison was over 200 (days) not out it had not yet closed its innings and he had better try to get a change of bowlers![25]

On 12th May the Mafeking "wicket" almost fell as Eloff and 300-odd Boer commandos launched the much feared and anticipated attack on the enervated garrison. The purely military events have been discussed earlier (see Chapter 2). It is worth, however, recalling key episodes to illustrate both the traumatic personal and individual experiences of this last major struggle for survival and the hitherto neglected role of the African auxiliaries who again demonstrated heroism equal to that of their white compatriots as well as an extraordinary capacity for all-out merciless revenge against their hated Boer enemy. The attack can be separated into three distinct phases. The first comprised the surprised foray into the town via the African stadt and the capture by Eloff, of the BSAP Fort including Colonel Hore and 22 BSAP at around 5.50 am. Secondly, the counter offensive when Baden-Powell conducted a stoic defence directing Major Godley, another hero of the Siege to cut off Eloff in the Fort and round up the increasingly isolated Boer outposts within the stadt. Finally, there was the final phase comprising the recapture of the BSAP Fort and the controversial "mopping up operations" that followed.

During the first phase the huge shock delivered to an already severely weakened Mafeking garrison was graphically evident. Widespread panic ensued amongst both black and white Mafeking citizens. Ada Cock, recalled those terrible moments at around 4 am on Saturday 12th May:

'It has been an awful morning—somehow the enemy have got into the BBP [BSA Police] camp about 500 yards from here... Willie and all of us got up at 4.30, hearing terrible firing and bugles blowing.... Soon, one end of the stadt was blazing and the niggers running and screaming... '[26]

Lady Wilson feared the worst as Mafeking's defences were suddenly so dangerously exposed.

'The Boers in the stadt! Such was the ominous message that quickly passed around... as day was breaking. One had to be well acquainted with the labyrinth of rocks, trees, huts and cover generally... all within a stone's throw of our dwelling to realize the dread import of these words... the moon had just set and it was pitch dark. The firearm fusillade first began from the east and when I opened the door on to the step the din was terrific, while swish, swish came the bullets just beyond the cover blinds nailed to the edge of the veranda to keep off the sun. Now and then the boom of a small gun varied the noise but the rifles never ceased for an instant! To this awe-inspiring tune I dressed by the light of a carefully-shaded candle to avoid giving any mark for our foes.... In various stages of deshabille the people were running around the house searching for rifles, fowling pieces and even sticks as weapons of defence'[27].

Baillie witnessed the terrible scenes in the stadt as Baralong men, women and children were ruthlessly shot down and up to 40 huts set alight. 'Suddenly on the west a conflagration was seen and betting began as to how far out it was. I got onto the roof of a house, and with Mr Arnold, saw a very magnificent sight... the whole stadt was on fire and with sunrise behind us and the stadt in flames in front, the combination of effects was magnificent, if not exactly reassuring!'[28]

Ross testified to the intensity of Boer rifle fire:

'Bullets fell like hailstones all over the town, the Market Square at times having the appearance of being lit up with electric sparks caused by explosive bullets or the Mauser bullet striking bits of stone or flint... I shall never forget the run I had from our place in this Market Square to the fort I was attached to at Early's Corner. How I dodged those bullets God alone knows. They were under me, over me, all around me, so I suppose I was meant for something else'[29].

In these desperate moments even the town jail, 400 yards from the BSAP fort, was emptied with prisoners including convicted murderer Lieutenant Murchison and convicted black marketeer, Sergeant Looney issued with rifles, the only predictable exception being the three Dutch prisoners. Ross thus encountered on the roof, 'poor old Murchison firing away for all he was worth with an old Martini rifle we had taken from one of the police prisoner guards. He, at any rate, was pleased at his temporary liberty and said he did not care a d...whether he was shot or not'[30].

At this critical time between 5 and 7.30 pm Baden-Powell again demonstrated his exceptional military leadership by swiftly and coolly establishing order and rapidly reorganizing the defences to close the dangerous gap caused by the Boer incursion. In this second phase of the battle, Major Godley emerged as yet another garrison hero, as, under telephoned orders from Baden-Powell, he courageously led units of the Protectorate Regiment, BSAP, and elements of the Cape Police from the Brickfields and Canon Kopje to re-establish the broken defence lines and cut off the captured BSAP Fort and Eloff's withdrawal route. Godley described his desperate ride to link-up with these reassembled units and thus plug the gap. As 'officers were galloping around everywhere', Godley recalled, 'my difficulty was to get the squadrons assembled ... I decided that the best thing to do was to concentrate as best we could on the south side of the stadt and then drive in from east and west and so cut off those Boers who had got into the fort from the parties who had remained in the stadt. It was a desperate ride as, 'to get to the rendezvous I had to go out in front of our defences and gallop around across the Molopo River and outside the stadt. After I had crossed the river I was well sniped at from the stadt, but I had managed to keep my pony (one of the few remaining in the garrison in fairly good condition) and made my pace so fast that I evidently presented a rather difficult running target; the bullets whistled either over or behind me. Our drive was entirely successful'[31].

The considerably grimmer final phase of the battle now began. The last stands of the now surrounded Boers in the stadt were mostly only overcome after furious firefights. The confidence of the garrison's defenders rapidly returned. Baillie witnessed 'bodies of men, individuals, everybody armed with what they could get, guns of any sort, running towards the firing, a smile on every man's face and the usual remark was, "now we've got the beggars"'[32]. Small units of Boers, often laden with loot, made desperate attempts to escape. Baillie again noticed 'one clumpy' of Boers who 'galloped forth laden with food and drink. The food belonged to them; the drink belonged to us. They happened to fall in with a galloping maxim, a piece of bad luck because they all died and our people took the food and drink. One fellow had taken a pair of brown boots and a horse; he had a few bullets through the boots, the horse was killed and so was he'[33]. A steady trickle of captured Boer wounded arrived at the garrison's field hospitals. Nurse Craufurd's heroic work has been earlier recorded, but Lady Wilson also bore witness to the 'gruesome sight seeing the wounded brought in and the bloody stretchers carried away empty' while the wounded Boer prisoners 'begged not to have sheets, as they had never seen such things before'. It was left to Lady Wilson to comfort one of the few garrison casualties, the mortally wounded Staff Orderly Hazelrigg of the Cape Police. As he 'bled to death' ... I sat with him several hours putting eau de cologne on his head and brushing away the flies. In the evening just before he passed into unconsciousness, he repeated more than once "Tell the Colonel, Lady Sarah, I did my best to give the message, but they got me first". He died at dawn'[34].

Hazelrigg's valiant death in a desperate attempt to carry Baden-Powell's messages to beleaguered parts of the garrison had an equally profound effect on Baden-Powell as had McLaren's grievous wounding earlier in the Siege (see Chapter 2). It reinforces the more plausible explanation that Baden-Powell's bond with these men was based on military comradeship and shared duty rather than any suggested implications of homosexuality.

It was at this stage of the attack that the African contribution, particularly by the Baralongs in the stadt area, became evident. They played a courageous role in both isolating and overwhelming the last Boer defenders. Baden-Powell himself noted how 'the Baralong had acted as scouts and found out where the remaining [Boers] had posted themselves'[35]. Baillie gave enormous credit to the Baralong support in isolating scattered Boer positions, singling out for particular praise the efforts of Lekoko and Silas Molema who had tactically decided that it was 'better to kraal them [the Boers] up like cattle'[36]. He noted; 'this species of fighting particularly appeals to the Baralong. He is better than the Boer at the Boers' own game and never will I hear a word against the Baralong'[37].

Thus, with the help of the already rearmed Baralong scouting guide, it was soon discovered that 30-odd Boer fighters were penned-up in a stone kraal and 50-odd in a rocky limestone koppie. In the final capture of these two main positions the Baralong again played a significant, if somewhat ominous, role. Two dozen Boers hemmed-in at the koppie surrendered under Major Godley's final threat of instant death (the garrison's seven-pounder gun had been lined-up at point blank range!) At that moment, a Captain Marsh 'at fearful risk jumped in amongst them and interposed himself between the cowering Boers and their would-be murderers'[38]. The hunger of the garrison troops was immediately evident as the captured enemy haversacks, with four days' rations of bread and biltong, were 'soon made short work of'[39]. The Boer kraal position met a similar fate. They surrendered at the point of the bayonet just before dark.

With no Captain Marsh to save them other smaller even more isolated Boer groups trapped between the stadt and the river by the angry and vengeful Baralong were less fortunate. Their terrible fate has been left largely unrecorded by contemporary historians and even at the time was kept secret, as the following description will reveal. After assessing the final Boer roll call of 17 dead, 109 prisoners and 19 wounded, (out of a 300 strong force), Snyman wrote to enquire about another 70 men missing![40] In a description reminiscent of the 1838 Piet Retief massacre when a 60-strong Boer commando was butchered by the Zulu, Ross revealed their similarly horrendous fate:

> 'As a matter of fact our natives got amongst a small crowd of them in the native village and using their small wood-chopping axes soon made mincemeat of them and the pieces of them may now be found in the river. All this is, of course, kept private but it was said it was impossible to restrain the natives once they got amongst them, as they said they were only doing to the Boer what the Boers had done to them and their women'[41].

It is probable that Baden-Powell and other senior commanders also knew about these excesses but, in the light of their professed beliefs in the concept of a "gentlemen's war", as well as awareness of justified Baralong grievances, they would have been unwilling to publicize such an incident. A cryptic observation of the scenes in the aftermath of the battle, however, shows how Baden-Powell may well have known something of their fate. Noting that the 'enemy's ambulance and search parties were out during the night picking-up in front of our outposts' ... he continued 'our patrols reported blood spoor, arms and ammunition haversacks lying about in quantities so that the losses had evidently been heavy'[42]. Baillie also spoke of up to 100 Boer bodies that 'will never be accounted for because the bodies of men with rifles may be possibly put away by the Baralongs'[43].

With the collapse of the Boer outposts in the stadt the fate of the Boer-occupied BSAP fort was also not long delayed. Baillie noted how Eloff, the Boer Commandant, had great difficulty in keeping his men together, some 100 earlier breaking away and escaping from the fort in spite of Eloff actually firing upon them. Hamilton captured earlier during the struggle and incarcerated in the Fort reported on the final moments:-

'Commandant Eloff called out "Surrender! Surrender!" and endeavoured strenuously to pacify his men. We upon our part shouted to the town to cease-fire; this was at once done whereupon the 67 Boers laid down their arms, handing them to the prisoners, who piled them up within the storehouse. Those of us who were not engaged in this work seized rifles and bandoliers from the heap and manned the defences of the fort until the prisoners could be delivered into proper custody. The Boers were then marched off and were found accommodation in the Masonic Hall and in the jail'[44].

For some of the Mafeking inhabitants this deadly face-to-face confrontation with their Boer foe had been a revelatory and emotional experience. In Baillie's words:

'We had never before seen a dead or wounded Boer or a prisoner, and it is weary work to see your friends and neighbours shot and not to see your own bag too, but personally, except in the way of business, I hope I haven't killed a Boer"[45].

For the many Boer prisoners the final surrender was itself a humiliating experience as Baden-Powell assigned 20 Fingos, "to assist in guarding prisoners" and, while the 'Britishers marked a respectful silence... the natives however hooted'[46].

There were many black and white heroes in this final battle, but it is notable that several diarists, many of whom had been critical of other aspects of Baden-Powell's leadership, were united in their praise of his particular military performance. Thus Ross, while admitting that 'the other side of the man is open to much argument', paid a typical fulsome tribute:

'The morning of 12th [May] was, of course, the first opportunity any of us had had of seeing BP in a temporary corner or at all hard pressed. And I can assure you it was indeed a lesson to all who saw him. I had that luck. He stood there at the corner of his offices, the coolest of cucumbers possible, but his orders rattled out like the rip of a Maxim. He had taken in the position without a moments thought or hesitation, and when he knew his outposts had been passed through by the enemy, within 20 minutes he had formed an inner line of defence right across the front of the town, with men and guns in sufficient numbers to mow down any number of the enemy that would dare to attempt to cross the clear open space still remaining between where the enemy were and the town. You could not realize his commands if put down in cold black and white. It was his tone, his self-possession, his command of self, his intimate knowledge of every detail of the defences, where everything at that moment was, and where it was to be brought and put to, showed us the ideal soldier, and what the British officer can be and is in moments of extreme peril. It was something I would not have missed seeing for anything. With only one or two with him, his officers all galloping about delivering his orders, there he stood with his hands behind his back, a living image of a being knowing himself and his own strength and fearing neither foe nor devil. Such was BP the soldier'[47].

The Eloff attack represented the Boers' "last card", the fiercest engagement since the Game Tree battle of December 1899. However, the strength, determination and ferocity of the Boer attack was a further testimony to how important Mafeking was perceived to be to them in military and particularly political terms. Five days later the relief force at last arrived to a joyous welcome.

In the intervening period Mafeking eyewitnesses excitedly observed the steady evacuation by the Boers of their surrounding laagers and forts. Mr Algie noted the great excitement prevailing on 14th May, as 'one large Boer group moved about the Southern Rise', the south-western Laager being 'vacated altogether' during the night[48]. As Colonel Mahon's 1,000 strong relief force closed in, Nurse Craufurd was moved to a more poetic observation; 'the great black mass by the laager seemed to divide itself and glide away in all directions and the veldt, before so quiet, was soon alive with horsemen'[49].

Ecstatic scenes greeted the spearhead troops of Mahon's column which had marched 250 miles in less than a fortnight, meeting Plumer about seven miles west of Mafeking and, 'absolutely confounding the Boers by their rapidity'[50]. The first arrivals, a lead squadron of Imperial Light Horse Infantry under Major Kerri-Davis received an initially muted welcome arriving rapidly in the middle of the night and only after several false alarms. A greatly surprised Lady Wilson was one of the first to greet him in the gathering gloom as she was roused at her dinner by:

> 'some feeble cheers. Thinking something must have happened I ran to the market square and seeing a dusty khaki-clad figure whose appearance was unfamiliar to me, I touched him on the shoulder and said, "Has anyone, come in?" "We have come in," he answered—Major Kerri-Davis and eight men of the Imperial Light Horse. Then I saw that officer himself and he told us that profiting by one hour's dusk they had ridden straight in before the moon rose and that they were now sending back two troopers to tell the column the way was clear'[51].

As word spread, however, these weary troopers were suddenly 'surrounded, besieged with questions, clapped upon the back, shaken by the hand and generally welcomed... Major Kerri-Davis called for cheers for the garrison while the crowd took up with tremendous fervour the National Anthem and Rule Britannia. It was an exciting moment and a picturesque scene bathed in soft moonlight and irradiated by the glow of countless stars'⁵².

The main column's arrival a few hours later sparked off even wilder scenes of jubilation. Filson Young, an officer in the Relief Forces' lead units, described the initially highly emotional scenes as:

> 'We galloped in over trenches, past breastworks and redoubts and little forts until we pulled up at the door of the headquarters mess.... No art could describe the handshaking and the welcome and the smiles on the faces of these tired-looking men; how they looked with rapt faces at us commonplace people from the outer world as though we were angels; how we all tried to speak at once, and only succeeded in gazing at each other and in saying, "By jove!" "Well I'm hanged!" and the like senseless expressions that sometimes mean much to Englishmen. One man tried to speak then he swore; then he buried his face in his arms and sobbed. We all gulped at nothing, until someone brought in cocoa and we gulped that instead; then Baden-Powell came in, and one could only gaze at him and search in vain on his jolly face for the traces of seven months' anxiety and strain'⁵³.

It was a night noisily celebrated by the black citizens of Mafeking who had contributed so much to the survival of the garrison. In her hospital Nurse Craufurd was kept wide-awake listening 'to the noise of the Baralongs celebrating the relief. Poor creatures, they had suffered fearfully during these seven-and-a half months, but had been loyal and brave through all'⁵⁴. As the main relief column arrived the real celebrations began. Hamilton again provides a vivid description of the scenes of jubilation.

> ...'About two in the morning a subdued roar came from the direction of the north-west outposts and, in a very little

time word was passed round that the troops were making their entrance into Mafeking. ...The town had aroused itself and was soon flocking across the veldt to the ground where the combined columns had already begun to form their camp. It was not a large force; its full muster was below 2,000; but amid the soft and eerie shadows of the starry, moonlit night, there seemed no end to the lines of horses, mules, and bullocks, to the camp fires, to the groups of men, to the number and variety of the waggons. In a corner, as it were, were the guns, a composite battery of the Royal Horse Artillery, eight pieces of the Canadian Artillery, and a number of maxims. It was these, which we had heard booming to us the first distant echoes of relief, and we were, of course, proud of them. Then and there we examined them, felt them over, pondered upon them, and then and there we thanked our god that we had in our own hands at least some really serviceable artillery. But there were other sights to be seen, early as was the hour, tired as were the troopers. There were the men of the Kimberley Light Horse and their comrades of the Imperial Light Horse to be inspected, to be patted upon the back, to be admired, and to be congratulated. ...Everyone seemed to be screaming, and as the Royal Horse Artillery swept through town we streamed after them, feebly endeavouring to keep pace with them, so as to be able to witness the effects of their power. The Market Square at this time presented a picture of military life that has never been equalled by any of the scenes that have been enacted there in its early days. Men in uniform were hurrying from point to point, troops from the various squadrons were coming in, squadron leaders, majors and colonels were falling over one another ...'[55]

Contrary to some of his critics, Baden-Powell had not been inactive during these final days and hours. As news arrived on 15th May of 500 Boers posted to 'receive Plumer's force' he prepared a small column of 220 men (including units of the Protectorate Regiment, BSAP, Cape Police and Bechuanaland Rifles) and two guns and a Maxim under Colonel Wexford 'to take the offensive; if necessary to create a diversion to help our relief'[56].

The arrival of the Canadian Artillery and their shelling of Game Tree fort in fact proved the final straw for the residual, defending Boer forces. The shelling continued for an hour led by the composite battalion of the Royal Horse Artillery's four 12½-pounders and two pom-poms and culminated in both garrison and relief forces advancing in skirmishing order. Lines were extended rapidly until Boer positions were out-flanked. In their panic to escape, even the Boer hospital and headquarters were abandoned leaving 30 Boer wounded to their fate. Perhaps showing awareness of what had earlier happened to their comrades at the hands of the vengeful Baralong, Baden-Powell rapidly posted a guard around the hospital. Game Tree Fort had earlier been abandoned, the Imperial guns 'terrorizing the Boers' who 'fled precipitately, leaving their camp, their guns, their stores, behind them'[57].

It was the signal for a mass-plunder of the Boer camps by white and black, civilian and military alike. An astonished Lady Wilson, 'had the experience of seeing a "loot" in progress. First we saw two soldiers driving a cow; then some more with bulged-out pockets full of live fowls; natives were staggering under huge loads of food stuffs, and eating them as they walked![58]' Whole waggon loads of Boer food were ransacked as if to compensate for the terrible past months of virtual starvation. Baden-Powell himself gazed upon 'several waggon loads of food stuffs and ammunition abandoned with all the Boer trenches hurriedly evacuated and food, clothing, arms, blankets, etc left behind in profusion'[59]. McMullen's camp became a special target and was duly 'searched for food and souvenirs of the Boers'[60].

Leading citizens were not averse to acquiring private loot. Ross himself took a return six-mile walk to the Boer main laager to get his share of the booty: 'We went out and we came back loaded down with all sorts of good things. I managed to secure myself a bag of flour and my pockets were crammed full of biltong, a flask of whisky found under one of the beds and a lot of other curios. Quite enough to carry for a three mile tramp home again!⁶¹'

As the looting subsided, time was made for the more sombre task of paying respects to the dead and offering thanksgiving. On 19th May the whole garrison paraded at the cemetery where, after a ceremony conducted by the Reverend Weeks, a Protectorate Regiment firing party fired three volleys over the graves of their dead comrades. A thanksgiving service was also held, the Colonel speaking personally to each detachment in turn. On this day the Town Guard was officially disbanded.

The Mafeking celebrations were mirrored, indeed far surpassed by the ecstatic reaction at home. The whole country dissolved into a delirium of joyfulness, the grand "Mafficking", thus adding a new word to the English language. After the desperately gloomy events of the last seven months, only temporarily relieved by the British victory at Paardeberg, (February 1900), the Relief had unleashed a cathartic explosion of emotion affecting all classes of people and practically every town and village in Britain. As the *Times* confirmed, on Saturday May 19th 1900, 'by common consent a public holiday had arranged itself'[62]. It underlined how important Mafeking had become as a psychological symbol, a veritable beacon of hope for the empire far beyond its intrinsic military value. Just as the heroic defence of Rorke's Drift (in which an unprecedented eleven VCs were awarded) compensated for the earlier disaster to British arms at Isandlwana and Omdurman substituted for the fall of Khartoum and the death of General Gordon, so the Relief of Mafeking made up for the devastating military blunders of "Black Week".

Never before in Britain's history had such a wave of patriotic hysteria swept the nation and not even the armistice celebration of 1918 or VE Day in 1945 were to equal the scale and extent of the celebration. Within five minutes of the news arriving at 9.17 pm on May 18th crowds of up to 20,000 surrounded the Mansion House in London singing the National Anthem. The frantic

Saturday scenes were described by one eye witness: 'White-haired old ladies were to be seen carrying large union jacks in each hand, and young women had colours pinned across from shoulder to shoulder. Sober-looking young men in spectacles stood at street corners blowing tin trumpets with all their might... Well-dressed young women of unusually proper demeanour traversed roadways, arm-in-arm, six abreast, carrying flags and occasionally bursting into song. There was a singular absence of any official stimulus'[63]. The spontaneity of the response was graphically illustrated by scenes even within the normally staid Stock Exchange, the financial powerhouse of empire. The work of both members and clerks was abandoned as groups shook hands and sang patriotic songs, and with much fervour the National Anthem. Such euphoria was repeated all over the Empire. In Canada a correspondent reported that 'every town and village went wild with patriotic fervour'. In Melbourne, Australia, guns were fired, bells rang all day and crowds packed the streets. In the midst of all the celebrations Baden-Powell emerged as the greatest British hero since Wellington and Nelson. It was five days before the country was able to return to normal[64].

Back in South Africa 'Mafficking' was taking a far more sinister form as, in the aftermath of the Siege, the black defenders of Mafeking and their local allies proceeded to exact a swift revenge on both the retreating Boer commandos and their African allies. For a brief while all of Snyman's and Cronje's earlier expressed fears and the nightmare scenario of a "racial Armegeddon", seemed close to realization. As the Mafeking garrison's white citizens continued to celebrate, armed raiding parties of Baralong, many undoubtedly equipped with Mauser rifles captured from the Boers during the Eloff attack and the post-relief orgy of looting, rapidly moved out of the town to seek retribution. An early primary target was the rebel Baralong chief Abraham Metuba's village at Rietsfontein. He had actively supported the Boers during the Siege and allegedly killed several of the garrison's messengers.

On 19th May a band of 300 Mafeking Baralongs led by Wessels duly raided Metuba's Kraal, looting all his cattle, with Metuba and 15 of his headmen captured and brought in to be jailed. A trusty ally, the headman Saani, imprisoned by Metuba's pro-Boer group, was simultaneously rescued[65]. Baillie mused on this unusual situation and welcomed the rough justice meted out to these 'black traitors'.

'I suppose this is the first occasion in which one black man surrendered under a white flag to another. These Rietsfontein rebels have always been against the remainder of the Barolongs, and have invariably fought for the Boers since the disturbed relations between Briton and Boer have existed. I hope they will shoot Metuba, as his people's invariable cunning in stopping our runners has caused us great inconvenience, not to mention the numbers they have killed'[66].

Black on black violence was one thing; uncontrolled violence by armed blacks against whites escalating to the killing of the largely defensive Boers on outlying farms inextricably forced the Imperial authorities to intervene, if only to defend white order. By the end of May it was clear that the profusion of armed African bands in the region was posing a serious threat to overall white authority. As local Boers pleaded for protection, Baden-Powell himself was forced to act against his own black allies. On 26th May he accordingly instructed Colonel Plumer to formally warn the hitherto friendly chief Linchwe, 'that he must on no account invade Marico and that, if the Boers at Sequan wanted to surrender, he would assure their protection[67]. On the same day, Colonels Plumer, Edwards, and Gould-Adams were formally ordered, not only to take the surrender of local Boers but, also, to provide them with protection against 'natives invading the Transvaal'[68]. Three days later, on 29th May, Chiefs Linchwe and Kalifing were directly 'warned to restrain their men from looting'[69]. Racial clashes and confrontations soon escalated. By 31st May the panicking Landdrost at Lichtenberg had urgently requested Baden-Powell to take over the district as '100 armed natives were marching on the town'[70]. As the "racial genie" slowly emerged out of his lamp British and Boers alike were forced to hastily form a temporary "unholy alliance" to forestall a general race war.

By early June Baden-Powell had been reluctantly forced in to carrying out a sustained campaign of pacification and "reconquest", not only of his main Boer enemy and their African allies, but his own armed African auxiliaries. On $2^{nd}$ June, Baden-Powell ominously reported to General Roberts that while supplies were now plentiful, the 'only difficulties for the moment are bands of armed natives marauding' for which he was 'taking repressive measures'[71]. By $4^{th}$ June it was reported that, 'serious looting was taking place at Barberspan by Mafeking Baralongs'. The wider political ramifications of this local racial crisis was soon evident with the South African High Commissioner himself now becoming, 'very anxious about the matter'[72]. Consequently, Baden-Powell ordered the local Baralongs to hand-in all arms and to return to their kraals with Chief Lekoko also again told to warn his people.

Near Lichtenburg 30 'looting Baralongs' were apprehended by British General Hunter, and Baden-Powell was soon forced to establish small posts of troops throughout the country while mounted police on commandeered horses were dispersed about the border to stop the raiding and looting. It was not, however, a policy of all-out repression. Baden-Powell privately expressed considerable sympathy for the Baralong grievances and demonstrated his acute awareness of their previous loyal service. On $19^{th}$ June, for instance, he recommended to Lord Roberts that, 'a reward be made to the Barolong Chiefs for their loyalty and good service in the shape of 100 head of cattle to Chief Lekoko as well as to Chiefs Silas, Molema and Paul Manip'[73]. It was a policy actively supported by his grateful fellow Mafeking citizens. Baillie reflected on the Baralong plight and expressed deep sympathy for the reasons lying behind their attacks on Boer farms.

'I wonder if people at home realize in what a position our loyalists in Bechuanaland have been placed. If they didn't come in their own countrymen regarded them as rebels—if they did, they lost all they had. But by doing as they have done, that is by carrying on their business while exposed to all the contumely and insult the Boers could heap on them, with the possible loss of life as well as property, they have served their country as well as those who have taken up arms; because their houses have always been a safe place for runners to go to, and news about the doings of the Boers could be obtained from them. Besides, they know which of the Boers fought, and which didn't, and this fact now terrifies the rebels and keeps many quiet, who might not otherwise be so.[74]

Other leading "Mafekingites", in addition to Baden-Powell and Baillie, also participated in this "carrot and stick" policy of pacification. Thus, Weil, the Mafeking supply merchant personally delivered 200 bags of mealies 'to his friends the Baralong'[75]. Raiding expeditions soon diminished, Linchwe being one of the last Baralong Chiefs to be contained—but not until his "war parties" furiously raiding cattle near Pilansberg, 30 miles north, had 'killed one Boer boy and wounded two others'[76].

Thus, by the end of June all-out racial conflict had been narrowly averted as 4,000 Boer rifles and 1,000 "native guns" were confiscated by Baden-Powell's troops. Lord Roberts thus confirmed that the wholesale disarmament of the Transvaal African population had been 'absolutely necessary else unarmed Boers not safe'[77]. As racial order was rapidly restored Roberts added, with evident relief, 'We find in practice natives giving in arms quite willingly and the measure highly approved of by both Boer and British farmers'[78]. The disarmament of the Barolong had certainly taxed the imperial conscience, already acutely aware of their overall loyalty during the Siege and the brutal provocation they had received from the Boer besieging forces. As the High Commissioner had earlier informed Lord Roberts prior to disarmament:

'I have informed Mafeking that orders have been given for Linchwe people to be disarmed. I hope it may not be thought necessary to carry out this step, as it is totally contrary to the policies successfully pursued by myself and all my predecessors with regard to the Protectorate natives who are directly under the High Commissioner. The present is, I think, a particularly unfortunate time for such a step as the Protectorate natives ... have been most loyal during the war and have greatly assisted us'[79].

The aftermath of the Siege as much as the Siege itself had, therefore, been of significant political consequence with a short-lived but direct African challenge to local colonial order. In a sense this brief exhibition of African "independence" had been realized only through their extensive sacrifices during the Siege of Mafeking. In the event the Official History of South Africa's total casualty roll for Mafeking belied the extent of their losses. Sixty-five "natives" and 264 Baralongs were listed as killed or died of wounds but, to this figure, of course, must be added the several hundred African civilians who died from malnutrition or disease. Total white combatant losses were listed as 67, with the coloured contingents losing 25. The total casualties civilian and military, wounded, killed and missing, during the Siege were officially listed as 813 of all races[80]. Such statistics, however, ignored the clearly immense psychological pressures endured by black and white Mafeking citizens during this epic seven and a half-month siege.

---

1     Ross *Diary*, 29–30 April 1900.
2     Cock, 6 May 1900, *Petticoat in Mafeking*, p. 89.
3     Ross *Diary*, 10 May 1900.
4     Cock, 6 May 1900, *Petticoat in Mafeking*, pp. 88–89
5     Ross *Diary*, 6 May 1900.
6     B-Powell, 6 May 1900, Staff Diary.
7     Cock, 6 May 1900, *Petticoat in Mafeking*, p.89.
8     Ross *Diary*, 6 May 1900.
9     Ross *Diary*, 10 May 1900.

10  Chamber of Commerce to B-Powell, 27 Mar 1900 (incl. in Ross *Diary* 31 March 1900).
11  Plaatje, *Mafeking Diary*, p. 133.
12  Roberts to B-Powell, 9 April. B-Powell 20 April 1900, Staff Diary.
13  B-Powell, 20 April 1900, Staff Diary.
14  *Ibid.*
15  B-Powell, 21 April 1900, Staff Diary.
16  *ibid*
17  Godley, *Life of an Irish Soldier*, pp. 80-1.
18  B-Powell, 25 April 1900.
19  B-Powell, 2 May 1900.
20  Ross *Diary*, 10 May 1900.
21  *Ibid.*
22  Cock, 28 April 1900, *Petticoat in Mafeking*.
23  *Ibid*, 3 May 1900.
24  B-Powell, 1 May 1900, Staff Diary.
25  B-Powell, 30 April 1900, Staff Diary.
26  Cock, 12 May 1900, *Petticoat in Mafeking*, pp. 99–91.
27  Wilson, *South African ?*, pp. 204–5.
28  Baillie, 15 May 1900, *Siege*, p. 253.
29  Ross *Diary*, 13 May 1900.
30  *ibid.*
31  Godley, *Life of an Irish Soldier*, p. 81.
32  Baillie, 15 May 1900, *Siege*, p. 254.
33  *Ibid.*
34  Wilson, *South African ?*, pp. 208–9.
35  B-Powell, Staff Diary.
36  Baillie, 15 May 1900, *Siege*, p. 263.
37  *ibid.*
38  *Mafeking Mail*, 14 May 1900.
39  Ross *Diary*, 15 May 1900.
40  Ross *Diary*, 15 May 1900.
41  *ibid.*
42  B-Powell, 13 May 1900, Staff Diary.
43  Baillie, 15 May 1900, *Siege*, p. 265.
44  Hamilton, *Siege of Mafeking*, p. 309.
45  Baillie, 15 May 1900, *Siege*, p. 276–7.
46  Baillie, *ibid*, p. 266.
47  Ross *Diary*,16 May 1900.
48  Algie *Diary*, 14 May 1900.
49  Cruwfurd *Diary*, 17 May1900.
50  Wilson, *South African ?*, p. 215.

51 *ibid.*
52 Hamilton, *Siege of Mafeking*, p. 315.
53 F. Young, *The Relief of Mafeking* (Methuen 1900) pp. 264–5.
54 Craufurd *Diary*, 17 May 1900.
55 Hamilton, *Siege of Mafeking*, p. 315–17.
56 B-Powell, 15 May 1900, Staff Diary.
57 Hamilton, *Siege of Mafeking*, p. 318.
58 Wilson, *South African ?, p. 218.*
59 B-Powell, 13 May 1900, Staff Diary.
60 Algie *Diary*, 18 May 1900.
61 Ross *Diary*, 20 May 1908.
62 *The Times*, 21 May 1900.
63 *ibid.*
64 For a voluminous extended discussion of the "Mafficking" celebrations in Britain and throughout the Empire see Gardner *Mafeking*, pp. 199–207.
65 Baillie, 15 May, *Siege*, p. 284.
66 Baillie, 17 May, *Siege*, p. 285.
67 B-Powell to Plumer, 26 May 1900. Mafeking Archives—as compiled by A Renew (hereafter MA).
68 B-Powell to Plumer, Edwards, and Gould-Adams, MA.
69 Algie *Diary*, 29 May 1900.
70 *ibid*, 31 May 1900.
71 B-Powell to Roberts, 2 June 1900, MA.
72 Mahon to B-Powell, 4 June 1900, MA
73 B-Powell to Roberts, 19 June 1900, MA.
74 Baillie, 17 May, 1900, *Siege*, p.285.
75 *ibid* 19 May, p. 289.
76 B-Powell to Roberts, 23 June 1900, MA
77 Roberts to B-Powell, 27 June 1900, MA
78 *ibid*
79 High Commissioner to Roberts. Enclosed is Roberts to B-Powell 25 June 1900, MA
80 HMG: *History of the War in South Africa 1899-1902, Vol II*, p. 550.

The political and military importance of the Siege of Mafeking has been significantly under-estimated. In military terms it can be argued that the Siege did, in fact, create a major diversion of existing Boer forces and significantly undermined its early war effort. The Siege initially tied-down up to 8,000 Boer combatants, up to one-fifth of the total existing Boer armed strength in the autumn of 1899. Even after Cronje's departure in November and the significant reduction in the size of the besieging force, many more Boer patrols had to be continuously deployed to protect their farms against constant garrison raids which extended up to a 30 mile radius. The garrison at Mafeking proved to be a running sore in the "body politic" of the Transvaal Boer authorities.

The Siege was of even greater significance in psychological terms. As even Thomas Pakenham, an otherwise severe critic of Baden-Powell, has pointed out, 'Wars are ultimately about morale'. Baden-Powell and his resolute garrison had scored a great victory as they had 'not only given back Britain its self-confidence, but dealt the Boers a crushing psychological blow by denying them Mafeking, the symbolic birthplace of the

Raid. No other British commander in the war had done so much with so little'[1]. The unprecedented scenes of celebration throughout Britain, following a litany of imperial disasters, were a glowing testament to this irrefutable fact.

Baden-Powell emerged as a high calibre military leader and this was demonstrated clearly by his tactical handling of the Eloff attack, an achievement universally admired by his contemporaries. Similarly, there is no substantial evidence of Baden-Powell's alleged homosexuality; his friendships with several officers (not just McClaren) such as Hazelrigg, were clearly based on often long-standing military comradeship in the midst of considerable adversity.

In other ways the Siege was an important political watershed turning point in the course of the Anglo-Boer War. What had begun as an ostensibly "white man's war", had, confirming local Boer fears, rapidly developed into a multi-racial conflict with, as we have seen, serious implications for the post-Siege, indeed possibly post-war, social order. In the early weeks of the Siege, Baden-Powell had happily played the "race card" in order to demoralize his Boer opponents. It was perhaps ironic that he himself was to be haunted by the appearance of the dreaded "black spectre" during the troublesome weeks following the ending of the Siege. Some form of black challenge was perhaps inevitable. African Siege heroes, often sharing equal rations and military duties with their white counterparts, revelled in this new enhanced or elevated social status.

As early as January 1900, the logistical dependency of the white garrison upon their African collaborators and auxiliaries had become patently evident. Baralong livestock raids had been matched by the courageous activities of the African and coloured unarmed and armed auxiliaries such as the Cape Boys, who played a crucial role in the defence of key areas of Mafeking such as the Brickfields defence line. Angus Hamilton, the War Correspondent, paid fulsome tribute to the local Baralong community who, in the later stages of the Siege, constituted a vital garrison lifeline.

# Conclusion

'In a way we have been compelled to depend to no small extent upon the prowess of the local tribe. The Baralong have done well by us, and have served us faithfully, and with no complaint. They have fought for us; they have preyed upon the enemy's cattle so that the white garrison might have something better than horse flesh for their diet; they have manned the western defences of the Stadt and they have suffered severe privations with extraordinary fortitude'[2].

While some Africans had politically and even economically prospered as a result of the Siege, there were also, of course, many less fortunate African "victims". As we have seen, several hundred Africans perished from starvation and/or disease during the Siege period, particularly the months of January to March. While the ignorance, neglect and belated relief policies of the white authorities played a significant role in this tragedy, inter-ethnic rivalry in the form of Baralong exclusivity cannot be discounted as a factor in exacerbating the food crisis. While many of the itinerant Transvaal African refugee groups faced starvation, many of their established Baralong counterparts survived, even prospered, maintaining sizeable cattle herds and vegetable gardens through to the final days of the Siege.

This immensely contentious issue of African welfare brings us to a re-assessment of the role of the man in charge, Lord Baden-Powell. During his conduct of the Siege Baden-Powell, like many military leaders, was forced to take many harsh political decisions, of which the policy of the enforced evacuation of "alien" African groups remains the most controversial. It was never simply a brutal policy of "leave or starve". Baden-Powell was under immense psychological and military pressures outside his immediate control. His meticulous rationing plans were completely undermined by the telegraphed news received from Lord Roberts in February and again in early April significantly delaying relief.

The policy of evacuation was high risk but the success of earlier voluntary evacuations would have given him some hope for success. Moreover, he did make genuine attempts to mitigate any adverse affects of this exodus, providing both armed escorts and food supplies for the evacuees, as well as seeking Boer guarantees for their safe passage. In hindsight it was a blunder, but the product of Baden-Powell's naïveté and misjudgement rather than any concept of premeditated murder as recent critics have seemed to suggest.

After the disaster of the February exodus Baden-Powell, it must be remembered, never repeated an enforced mass evacuation policy again. Furthermore, he made positive efforts over the next two months to alleviate cases of acute starvation amongst the remaining Transvaal African groups, not only through his soup kitchen system, but also by *direct* interventions such as the rescue and feeding of up to 50 starving Shangaanis on the 15th April. On April 21st he even held a crisis meeting almost solely concerned with the problem of African food supplies and which resulted in directives to improve the quality and nutritious value of the kitchen soup supplies. Furthermore, he frequently rewarded African cattle-raiders and soldiers. These were not the actions of a "war criminal". Even radical contemporary critics such as Neilly gave him credit for the extensive remedial measures taken after the extent of the African food crisis had become clear.

Moreover, as Hamilton and other contemporary eyewitnesses have observed, Baden-Powell was an exceptionally busy distracted man, preoccupied, if not obsessed, with the garrison defences and military matters in general. He rarely visited the African stadt or soup kitchen areas and spent most of his time either in his headquarters office or "look-out position", or surveying by night and day, the external defence areas. African welfare was invariably left to subordinates to organize and administer.

Indeed, it is clear that malpractices and irregularities were carried out by some junior officers and officials, both controlling the soup kitchens and involved in the requisition of food. The humanitarian Colonel Hore, on at least one occasion, drew

# Conclusion

attention to this continuing problem at the lower levels of administration (see Chapter 8) and Plaatje himself made several cryptic and overt references to such junior administrators and their overall ignorance or intolerance of African customs and welfare needs[3]. Much has also been made of the six African executions which occurred during the Siege but these tragedies, spread over a seven-and-a-half month period, were comparatively rare and were not personally administered by Baden-Powell. The Court of Summary Jurisdiction was also invariably run by other senior officers.

If at times he was excessively harsh in his policies towards elements of the African population he could at times be equally severe towards the white community. White deserters were sentenced to death in absentia and would have been shot, if caught. His decision to move Dutch women and children into the line of Boer shellfire in January provides another example of this. Indeed, some of the more extreme attacks launched against him by his white critics were, if not motivated by envy, at least partly based on growing resentment at his increasingly authoritarian control over the *European* garrison. All the war correspondents, Mr Ross and even Mr Algie, had clashed with Baden-Powell on separate occasions. If, in overall terms his racial sympathies ultimately lay with the white community it was surely a not unexpected reflection of the prevailing racial prejudices of his time—he was stereotypical of his generation.

Notwithstanding this fact, the tragic deaths which occurred within Mafeking still pale into insignificance when compared with the newly discovered large-scale black "concentration camps" set-up later in the Boer war and, indeed, the enforced incarceration of thousands of *white* women and children in such camps under the "scorched earth" policy of Lord Roberts and General Kitchener. Such policies were to result in the cost of many more thousands of lives across the racial divide.

In summary, Lord Baden-Powell's policies during the Siege of Mafeking were no harsher, indeed arguably even less harsh, than the policies of many of his contemporaries towards African communities during the Anglo-Boer War. Like all prominent leaders, Baden-Powell had his faults—he could be vain, egotistical and, on occasions, stubborn and uncompromising, but his actions were invariably conditioned by military exigencies *not* by conscious or deliberate racism.

1   Pakenham, *Boer War*, p.417.
2   Hamilton, *Siege of Mafeking*, p.261.
3   As Plaatje tellingly observed, the African food supply arrangements were 'in the hands of young officers who know as little about natives and their mode of living as they know about the man on the moon and *his* mode of living'. Plaatje, *Mafeking Diary*, p.80.

# Select Bibliography

## Published primary/contemporary sources
Baden-Powell, R S S, *Lessons from the Varsity of Life* (Pearson, London, 1933).
Ibid, *Sketches in Mafeking and East Africa* (Smith Elder, London, 1907).
Baillie, F D, *Mafeking: A Diary of the Siege* (Constable, London, 1900).
Godley, R S, *Khaki and Blue* (Lovat Dickson & Thompson, London, 1935).
Godley, Sir Alexander, *Life of an Irish Soldier* (John Murray, London, 1939).
Hamilton, J A, *The Siege of Mafeking* (Methuen, London, 1900).
Midgley, J F, *Petticoat in Mafeking. The Letters of Ada Cock* (Cape Town, 1974).
Neilly, J E, *Besieged with B-P* (Pearson, London, 1900).
Stirling, J, *The Colonials in South Africa* (Blackwood, London, 1907).
Whalley, G F, *With Plumer to Mafeking* (London, 1900).
Willan, B, *Edward Ross, Diary of the Siege of Mafeking* (Cape Town, 1980).
Willan, B, Plaatje, S T, *Mafeking Diary* (Meridor Books, London 1973).
Wilson, Lady Sarah, *South African Memories* (Arnold, London, 1909).
Young, F, *The Relief of Mafeking* (Methuen, London, 1900).

## Unpublished primary sources
Baden-Powell, R S S, Staff Diary (October 1899 to May 1900) NAM.
Renew, A, Algie Diary (October 1899 to May 1900) and Baden-Powell and Roberts Correspondence MA.

## Contemporary articles, newspapers and periodicals
*Black and White Magazine* (esp Vols 2 and 29).
Craufurd; A M, *A Nurse's Diary* (*Crampton's Magazine*, 1900).

*Mafeking Mail* (October 1899 to June 1900).
*The Times* 1899-1900.
Wilson, H W (ed), *With the Flag to Pretoria* Vols I and II (Harmsworth, London, 1901).

**Contemporary and recent biographies**
Aitken, W F, *Baden-Powell: The Hero of Mafeking* (Partridge and Co, London, 1900).
Beghie, H, *The Wolf that Never Sleeps* (Richards, London, 1900).
Bremner Smith, R J, *Colonel R S S Baden-Powell* (London, 1900).
Fletcher, J S, *Baden-Powell of Mafeking* (Methuen, London, 1900).
Grinnell-Milne, D, *Baden-Powell at Mafeking* (The Bodley Head, London, 1957).
Hillcourt, W and (Lady) Olave Baden-Powell, *Baden Powell: The Two Lives of a Hero* (Heinemann, London, 1964).
Hopkins, P and Dugmore, H, *The Boy: Baden-Powell and the Siege of Mafeking* (Zebra Books, New Holland Struig, 1999).
Jeal, T, *Baden-Powell* (Hutchinson, London, 1989).
Kiernan, R H, *Baden-Powell* (Harrap, London, 1939).
Reynolds, E E, *Baden-Powell* (Oxford, 1942).
Rosenthal M, *The Character Factory* (Collins and Sons, London, 1986).
Smuts, J C, *Jan Christian Smuts by his Son* (Cassell, London, 1952).
Wade, E K, *The Piper of Pax* (Pearson, London, 1924).

**General histories**
Amery, L S (ed), *The Times History of the War in South Africa, Vols II and IV* (Sampson Low, London, 1902 and 1906).
Conan Doyle, A, *The Great Boer War* (Smith Elder and Co, London, 1901).
Gardner, B, *Mafeking* (Cassell, London, 1965).
Hamilton, General Sir Ian, *Listening for the Drums* (London, 1944).
Harding, C, *Frontier Patrols: History of the BSA Police* (Bell, London, 1937).
Headley, Cecil (ed), *The Milner Papers Vol I*, (Smith Africa, 1899); *Vol II* (South Africa 1899 - 1905) (London 1931, 1935).

*Select Bibliography* 169

Kruger, R, *Goodbye Dolly Gray, A History of the Boer War* (Cassell, London, 1959).
Le May, G H L, *British Supremacy in South Africa 1899-1907* (Oxford, 1965).
Nasson, W, *The South African War 1899 - 1902* (Arnold, London, 1999).
Pakenham, E, *Jameson's Raid* (Weidenfield and Nicholson, London, 1960).
Pakenham, T, *The Boer War* (Weidenfield and Nicholson, London, 1979).
Spiers, E M, *The Army and Society (1815 - 1914)* (London, 1980).
Warwick, P (ed), *Black People and the South African War* (CUP 1983).
*ibid, The South African War* (London, 1980).

# Index

## A
Abrahams, Sgt 104, 117, 136
Afghanistan 12
Albrecht, Maj 47
Algie 78, 96, 104, 107, 109, 112-114, 118-120, 122-123, 126, 130-133, 148, 159-160, 165
Anderson, Surgeon Maj 90
Arnold, Mr 142
Ashanti 5, 13-14
Ashanti Expedition 13

## B
Baden-Powell, Col R. S. S. 5-8, 11-14, 16-21, 23-24, 27-30, 32, 34-36, 38, 40-42, 44, 46-47, 50-51, 54, 57-58, 60-61, 63, 65-68, 70-71, 73-74, 76-77, 79-80, 82-86, 90-91, 93, 95, 99, 101-107, 109-111, 115, 116-118, 123, 125-128, 130-132, 136-141, 143-148, 150-157, 161-165
Baillie, Maj 12, 19-20, 35, 38, 44, 52-53, 58, 65, 77, 98, 109, 118-119
Baralong 22, 36, 41, 44, 53, 65-66, 80-81, 92-93, 100-101, 103-106, 110, 116-118, 121-123, 125, 133, 140, 142, 145-146, 150, 152, 154, 156-158, 162-163
Basutoland 3
Bechuanaland 5, 8, 16, 27, 31, 40-41, 45-47, 49, 55, 58-59, 63, 66, 76, 127, 151, 156
Bechuanaland Rifles (Volunteers) 31, 41, 47, 58-59, 63, 66, 76, 127, 151
Bell, Mr 20, 104
Black Watch 22, 41, 71, 73, 93, 104
Black Week 96, 106, 153
Bloemfontein 2, 5
Bloemfontein Convention 2
Blood River 2
Boy Scout Movement 23, 128
Brady, Lt 52
Bremont, Capt 68
Brickfields 17, 40, 51, 54-55, 57, 62-66, 75, 77, 84, 98, 104, 115, 128, 143, 162
British South Africa Police (BSAP) 10, 16-17, 33, 35, 40-42, 46, 50-51, 56, 58-59, 65-67, 76, 80, 98, 102, 136, 141, 143, 146, 151
Brown, Capt 43
BSAP Fort 33, 65-66, 141, 143
Buchan, Helen 32
Buchan, James 22
Bulawayo 5, 8, 14, 17, 26-28, 45, 49, 71, 90
Buller, Gen 25
Burt, Cpl 55
Butler, Lt-Gen Sir William 7

## C
Cadet Corps 23, 68, 128
Canadian Artillery 151
Cannon Kopje 16, 39-40, 42-43, 55-57, 66, 75, 80, 87, 97
Cannon Kopje Fort 66
Cape Boys 17, 22, 57, 62, 75, 77, 84, 98, 102, 104, 119, 125, 139, 162
Cape Colony 6, 8, 14, 31, 44, 46, 49
Cape Police 17, 35, 41-43, 45-46, 54-55, 57, 62-63, 66, 73, 98, 126, 143-144, 151
Cape *Times* 80
Carnarvon, Lord 3

# Index

Carrington, Sir Frederick  14
Cavendish-Bentinck, Capt Lord Charles  15, 25, 51-52, 60, 67, 77
Cavendish-Bentinck, Lady Charles  25
Cecil, Lady Violet  6, 25
Cecil, Maj the Lord Edward  4, 6-7, 9, 15, 23, 25, 49, 59, 68, 128, 138-139
Chamberlain, Joseph  4, 7
Cock, Ada  31, 78-79, 113, 123-124, 135-136, 140-141
Colonial Contingent  22, 41, 75
Concentration camps  1, 165
Convent  2, 4, 29, 32, 40, 42-43, 72-73, 107, 123
Cook, Tpr  136
Court House  72, 84-85
Cowan, Capt  58-59, 76
Cowan, Gunner  58
Cowan, Miss  33
Creeky (Creechy)  22, 24, 28, 73-74, 77-78, 96, 114
Crewe, Fred  17
Cronje, Gen  36, 50, 54, 57-59, 71-75, 77, 83, 99, 118, 154, 161
Currie, Cpl  17, 57, 62, 77, 88, 98

## D

*Daily Chronicle*  75
Dall, (Councillor)  22, 63, 97
Daniels, Lt  41, 66, 98
De Kock, J. W.  43, 102
Dowling, Surgeon Maj  90
Drakensberg  13

## E

Edwards  155, 160
Elandslaagte  80
Eloff, Cmdt Sarel  5, 33, 35, 64-66, 68, 135, 140-141, 143, 146-148, 154, 162

## F

Feltham, Lt  66, 114
Fingos  37, 80-81, 104, 109, 118, 147
Five Mile Bank  51, 71-72, 75
Flygare, Capt  75
Fort Ayr  43, 136
Fort Cardigan  43
Fort Cronje  99
Fort Miller  43
Fort Nelson  136
Fort Victoria  42
Franklin, Cpl  89
Fraser, Tpr  55
Free State artillery  47
Frere, Sir Bartle  3
Fuller, Emily  31
Fuller, Harry  31

## G

Gaboutloeloe, Cornelius  93
Game Tree Fort  28, 59-60, 64, 76, 84, 90-91, 95-96, 99, 106, 111, 116, 148, 151-152
Gardner, Brian  31, 120
Gerrans Mr  89
Girdwood, Capt  63
Godley, Lady  25
Godley, Lt  17
Godley, Maj  6, 8-9, 16-17, 24, 37, 41-43, 58, 60, 66-67, 75, 81, 91, 100, 139, 141, 143, 145
Goodyear, Capt  22, 57, 75
Goold-Adams, Maj  8, 16, 21, 45
Gordon, Gunner
Graham, Capt  14
Grayson  78, 120
Grayson, Mr  78
Great Trek  2
Grenadier Guards  6
Griqualand West  3

## H

Hamilton (Dr) 61
Hamilton, J. A. 9, 17, 44, 51-52, 54, 56-57, 59-62, 64, 67-69, 86, 94-95, 103-104, 106, 109, 112-114, 120, 124, 128, 130-133, 147, 150, 159-160, 162, 164, 166
Hanbury-Tracy, Lt the Hon Algernon 6
Hanbury-Tracy, Maj 35
Hanbury-Williams, Col 7
Harland, Lt 16
Hayes, (Dr Tom) 33, 61, 90
Hayes, (Dr William) 82
Hayes, Mrs 28
Hazelrigg, Staff Orderly 144
Hellawell, Mr 80
Hopkins, Pat 19
Hore, C. O. Col 6, 8, 20, 34-35, 47, 60, 65-68, 126, 141, 164
Hunter, Gen 156
Hussars, 13th 6, 11, 13-14, 19

## I

Imperial Light Horse Infantry 15, 149, 151
India 5, 12-14, 21, 85, 101
Intombe Drift 3
Isandlwana 3, 153

## J

Jackal Tree 56, 73, 119
Jameson Raid 4, 6, 8, 10, 15, 46, 50
Jameson, (Dr) 42, 49
Jeal, Tim 113, 120, 125, 132-133
Johannesburg 4, 15, 41, 71, 81, 122
Joseph, Sister 32

## K

Kalifing 155
Kanya 110
Kerri-Davis, Maj 149
Khartoum 153
Kiddy, Mr 74
Kimberley 5, 7, 25, 27, 80, 90, 125, 151
Klein Marico Fort 75
Kruger, President Paul 4-6, 9, 20, 22, 29, 46, 54, 57, 64, 70, 74-75, 77, 135

## L

Lake, Mrs 32, 52
Lancers, 13th 5
Lancs 6
Lekoko, Chief 103, 105, 113, 123, 125, 127, 133, 145, 156
Lichtenburg 74, 156
Limestone Fort 43, 91
Linchwe, Chief 155, 157
London 4, 14, 45, 113, 115, 153
Looney, Sgt-Maj 99
Louw, Cmdt 54
Lucknow 11-12

## M

Mackenzie, Mr 119, 136
Mafeking 5, 7-9, 11, 14-19, 21, 23-29, 31, 36-37, 39-41, 44-46, 49-50, 52, 55, 59, 64, 69, 71, 73, 76, 78, 80, 82-83, 86-87, 89-99, 106-108, 112-114, 117-118, 121, 123-124, 127-129, 131-143, 145, 147-151, 153-162, 165-166
*Mafeking Mail* 91, 127, 133, 159
Majuba Hill 4
Malta 13
Manip, Paul 156
Marsh, Capt 42-43, 45, 58, 145
Marsh, Inspector 62
Marsham, Capt the Hon D. 56
Masonic Hall 63, 147
Matabele 14, 16, 18, 46
Matabeleland Relief Force 16
Matron Hill 32

# Index

Matthews, Sgt  80
McDonald, Tpr  55
McLaren, Capt Kenneth  6, 12, 18, 19
Metuba, Abraham  154
Middleditch, Tpr  55
Milner, Sir Alfred  4, 6-7, 25-26
Moleloane (Village)  123
Molema, Silas  105, 145
Molopo River  36, 39, 143
Moncrieffe, Ronnie  23
More, Mrs  28
Morgan, Bugler  61
Murchison, Lt  18, 56, 68, 75, 78, 143
Murray, Lt  43, 54

## N

Natal  2, 5-6, 13, 18, 26
Natal Mounted Rifles  18
Neilly, J. E.  120-121, 131-132, 164
Nelson, the Lord (cannon)  41, 45, 98, 136, 154
Ngidi, Alfred  100

## O

Omdurman  153
Orange Free State  3-6, 47
Orange River  2-3

## P

Paardeberg  153
Pakenham, Thomas  110, 120, 161
Panzera, Maj  17, 41, 50, 60, 66, 98, 107, 115
Parslow, Mr  18, 68, 75
Paton, Lt  60-61
Pearson, Mr  27, 80
Pechell, Capt Charles  56
Perry, Mr  71
Phaal, Annie  35
Pilson, Maj  16
Piper, Tpr  98

Plaatje, Sol  39, 81, 83, 91, 93-97, 100-101, 103, 108-113, 117-119, 121-122, 124-127, 131-133, 158, 164, 166
Plumer, Col Herbert  6
Plumer, Lt-Col Herbert  6, 8, 14, 16, 18, 47, 110, 135, 139, 149, 151, 155, 160
Pretoria  4, 6, 48, 73, 78
Protectorate Regiment  8, 15, 17, 40, 42, 45, 47, 51-52, 54, 58-60, 63-67, 71, 73-75, 77, 84, 90-91, 114, 143, 151, 153

## Q

Queen Victoria (Great White Queen)  9-11, 82, 103
Quinlan  21, 71

## R

Railway Institute  28, 32, 62
Railway Volunteers  21-22, 32, 35, 42-43, 72, 78
Recreation Ground Fort  43
Reisle, Mrs  52
Renew, Audrey  21, 54
Reuters  27, 80, 82
Rhodes, Cecil  4, 49
Rhodesia  5-6, 8, 14, 17, 24, 26, 36, 44-47, 50
Rhodesia Regiment  47
Rietsfontein  154-155
Roberts, Lord  11, 75, 138, 156-157, 163, 165
Robinson, Sir Hercules  6
Rolt, Maj Peter  16
Ross, Edward  71-72, 76, 78-79, 82-83, 90-91, 94-95, 97, 99, 101-102, 105-106, 108, 111-113, 115-117, 119, 126, 131-136, 139-140, 142-143, 146-147, 152, 158-160, 165

# Index

Royal Fusiliers 6
Royal Horse Artillery 151-152
Royal Horse Guards 6, 16
Royal Irish Rangers 6
Royal Military College Sandhurst 11
Russell, Gen Sir Baker 6, 18
Ryan, Capt 99-100

## S
Salisbury, Lord 6, 15
Sand River 2
Sandford, Capt 60-61, 86
Scott, Sir Francis 13
Setlagoli River 64
Shangaanis 36-37, 80, 108, 120-122, 124-126, 164
Singleton, Capt 34, 65
Snyman, Gen 27, 36, 50, 59, 64, 66, 77, 85, 93, 104, 118, 146, 154
Soundy, Tpr 55
Stanislaus, Sister Mary 72, 82
Stent, Vere 82
Stevens, Pte 73
Stewart, Mr 120
Stirling, Col 21
Stirling, Col J. 9, 21, 45, 47, 52, 69

## T
Taylor, Sgt-Maj 116
*The Morning Post* 38
*The Times* 160
Tiffin, Sgt-Maj 76
Town Guard 21-22, 31, 41, 43, 66, 72, 76, 89, 153
Transvaal 3-6, 8-9, 37, 47-49, 70-71, 77, 105, 110, 120-122, 126-127, 155, 157, 161, 163-164
Turner, Tpr 55

## U
Uitlanders 4, 15, 120
Ulundi 3

## V
Vaal 2, 44
Vere, Mr 121
Vernon, Capt 42, 58-61, 90
Victoria Cross 16, 75
Victoria Hospital 28, 32, 35, 72, 76
Von Weismann, Capt 68
Vyvyan, Lt-Col 8, 41

## W
Walford, Col 42, 56
Warren, Sir Charles 16, 39, 45
Webb, Tpr 73
Webster, Mr 22, 104
Weeks, Rev 153
Weil, Ben 76, 90, 94
Weil, Julius 94
Wenham, Mr 78, 119
Werner, Mrs 28
Wesley, Richards 118
Wessels, Chief 36, 103-104, 154
Wexford, Col 151
Whales, Mr 91
Whelan, Mr 21, 71
Whiteley, Mr 20, 41
Williams, Capt 59, 65, 115
Wilson, Capt Gordon 8, 25-26
Wilson, Lady Sarah 8-9, 19, 24-26, 29, 32, 37, 45, 62, 80, 89-90, 107, 122, 142, 144, 149, 152
Wolseley, Lord 5-7, 11, 14, 18, 44

## Y
Yorks 6
Young, Filson 150
Young, Mr 34

## Z
Zulu War 16
Zululand 14

# WELCOME TO COVOS-DAY BOOKS

## Southern Africa's newest publishing house

In late 1997, in Johannesburg, Covos-Day Books began life as a part-time, "mailorder-from-home" business – with one title. We soon appreciated that the southern African market was not being adequately serviced in terms of non-fiction – military, historical and socio-political material. In a short space of time, we have established ourselves as a leading African publisher in these fields. This year, 2000, we publish 14 new titles. We are now expanding into international markets and our books are being enthusiastically received.

To date, our focus has been the Anglo-Boer War and the southern African "bush wars" of the 1970s and 1980s. However, this year we shall also be developing other categories, including southern African fiction, literature and auto/biography. Without losing sight of our core business, we are, however, not afraid to explore other diverse and exciting areas – from war poetry – to accounts of Japanese POWs in World War II – and ANC exiles during the Apartheid era.

The publishing business in Africa is alive and well – producing top quality books that are vibrant, entertaining and historically relevant. Keep an eye out for our titles!

---

Prices indicated in this catalogue are recommended retail prices in South Africa, United Kingdom, USA, Canada, Australia and New Zealand.

Prices may vary slightly and are subject to change without notice.

Book specifications and publication dates are, in some instances, provisional.

## COVOS-DAY BOOKS

P. O. Box 6996
Weltevredenpark, 1715
South Africa

tel +2711-475 0922
fax +2711-475 8974
email: covos@global.co.za
website at **www.mazoe.com**

Design by **JANT Design**, Centurion, South Africa.
email: j.design@mweb.co.za

# NEW TITLES

## BELOVED AFRICAN
*Jill Baker*

The author, among Zimbabwe's, previously Rhodesia's, best-loved media personalities, writes about her enigmatic father, John Hammond, one of that country's earliest and foremost educators. A pioneer at the turn of the century, he helped forge the solid educational system that spawned some of the great minds of the country, including many of the founding black nationalists. A controversial, but much-loved figure.

**In the same vein as "Cry the Beloved Country"**

*Hardback; 228 x 155mm; 508 pages; 58 b/w photographs, map; 0 620 24117 9*

**R165.00**   £20.00   US$30.00   C$40.00   A$40.00   NZ$55.00

---

## VLAMGAT – The Story of the Mirage F1 in the South African Air Force
*Brigadier Dick Lord*

The sequel to *Fire, Flood and Ice*, this is an outstanding compilation of stories and experiences of SAAF Mirage pilots who operated in the Angolan and the SWA/Namibian bush wars. The author, an ex-Top Gun and Fleet Air Arm pilot, was at one time the CO of 1 Squadron (Mirages), the SAAF. A thrilling account told "from the cockpit".

*Hardback; 228 x 155mm; 380 pages; 55 colour, 169 b/w photographs, maps, diagrams; 0 620 24116 0*

**R185.00**   £20.00   US$35.00   C$45.00   A$45.00   NZ$60.00

---

## BOMBARDMENT OF LADYSMITH ANTICIPATED
### – The Diary of a Siege
*Alan Chalmers*

Into the cauldron of the siege of Ladysmith arrived the slight, Chaplinesque figure of George Maidment, a British Army orderly, fresh out from the Midlands of England. For over 100 days he recorded the events of the siege in his diary – the daily tedium, the fighting, the sniping, the lack of food, the disgust at eating their own horses. One bungled relief attempt after another as the great British Army was put through its paces by a bunch of farmers. This is a story of great courage lying alongside great stupidity, of world events alongside the personal, intimate observations of a local boy.

*"Of the myriad books published for the Anglo-Boer War Centenary this is one of the best illustrated and most well written"* – Meurig Jones, Chairman, Victorian Military Society

*Softback; 222 x 152mm; 340 pages; 298 b/w illustrations; 9 foldout maps; 0 620 24996 X*

**R140.00**   £15.00   US$25.00   C$35.00   A$35.00   NZ$45.00

# NEW TITLES

## WE FEAR NAUGHT BUT GOD
*Paul Els*

The story of the South African Special Forces ("The Recces"), from inception in the 1960s to disbandment in 1993. A unique account of one of South Africa's premier units, masters in the art of reconnaissance and clandestine warfare. Pro rata, the most highly decorated unit during the wars in Angola and Namibia/SWA.

*Includes a free copy of Lourens Fourie's music CD "The Recces"*

*Softback; 222 x 152mm; approx. 320 pages; approx. 200 b/w illustrations, maps 0 620 23891 7*

**R140.00**  £15.00  US$25.00  C$35.00  A$35.00  NZ$45.00

---

## FIRE IN THE SKY – The Destruction of the Orange Free State 1899-1902
*Owen Coetzer*

A shocking account of Britain's official Boer War policy of scorched earth, farm burning and concentration camps. "More than 27,000 people", mainly women and children, died in appalling conditions. It was a mistake, Milner later wrote. But a brutal one, the consequences of which are still felt today. An in-depth, horrifying exposé.

*Softback; 222 x 152mm; 383 pages; 49 b/w photographs, map; 0 620 24114 4*

**R120.00**  £15.00  US$25.00  C$35.00  A$35.00  NZ$45.00

---

## MAFEKING!
*Malcolm Flower-Smith and Edmund Yorke*

Psychologically affected by the fact that it was from Mafeking that the Jameson Raid was launched, the Boers determined to regain this key town. The exceptional military leadership, indomitable spirit and personal charisma of Colonel Baden-Powell made him the ideal officer for the British defence – the source of inspiration for the defenders of Mafeking during the epic 7½-month siege. By March 1900, the garrison was famished; death and destruction had become daily fare. When, in May, Mafeking was finally relieved, the British nation was swept by a wave of patriotic hysteria, unequalled since.

*With the foreword by The Honourable Mrs Betty Clay CBE, daughter of Lord Baden-Powell*

*Softback; 222 x 150mm; approx. 185 pages; approx. 48 b/w illustrations; 0 620 25251 0*

**R100.00**  £10.00  US$17.50  C$25.00  A$25.00  NZ$32.50

# CURRENTLY AVAILABLE

## PAMWE CHETE – The Legend of the Selous Scouts
*Lieutenant-Colonel Ron Reid-Daly*

The revamped, rewritten version of the best-selling *Top Secret War*. With new, previously unpublished material, including the roll of honour and full schedules of citations and wings. New photo sections. The definitive account of this exceptional unit's short but distinguished service in the field of pseudo counter-insurgency operations during the bitter Rhodesian bush war. A classic.

*Hardback; 228 x 155mm; 664 pages; 150 b/w illustrations, maps; 0 620 23756 2*

| **R225.00** | £27.50 | US$45.00 | C$60.00 | A$60.00 | NZ$75.00 |

---

## FIREFORCE – One Man's War in the Rhodesian Light Infantry
*Chris Cocks*

Widely acclaimed as the classic account of counter-insurgency warfare in Africa, as told by the combat soldier "on the ground". The gut-wrenching account of brutal face-to-face combat in the bush, this is not for the squeamish. Has been compared with *Commando* and *Dispatches*. Includes the RLI roll of honour, citations and operational orders, as appendices.

*"A tour de force"* – Paul Moorcraft

*Hardback; 228 x 155mm; 368 pages; 120 b/w & colour photographs; map/sketches; 0 620 21573 9; $2^{nd}$ Edition; Reprinted 1998, 1999, 2000*

| **R185.00** | £20.00 | US$35.00 | C$45.00 | A$45.00 | NZ$60.00 |

---

## ECHOES OF AN AFRICAN WAR
*Chas Lotter*

A photographic anthology by Africa's acclaimed soldier-poet. Coffee-table format with alternative pages of haunting poetry, mirrored by some stunning original photography. Also a 150 leather-bound, gilded Limited Edition.

*"…only the poets of the First World War have captured so compellingly the many moods of the young soldiers"* – Professor Marcia Leveson, President of the English Academy of Southern Africa.

*Hardback; 330 x 248mm; 208 pages; 650 colour photographs; 0 620 23091 6*

| Standard: | **R295.00** | £30.00 | US$50.00 | C$75.00 | A$75.00 | NZ$100.00 |
| Limited: | **R995.00** | £100.00 | US$175.00 | C$250.00 | A$250.00 | NZ$325.00 |

# CURRENTLY AVAILABLE

## SURVIVAL COURSE
*Chris Cocks*

The sequel to the best-selling *Fireforce*. Chronicling the author's 15-month experience, up to Zimbabwean independence in 1980, as a stick-leader in the specialist PATU (Police Anti-Terrorist Unit), operating on Rhodesia's eastern border. Part Two of the book deals with the author's traumatic and harrowing transition to civilian life in post-war Zimbabwe.

*Softback; 222 x 152mm; 244 pages; 40 b/w photographs, map; 0 620 24115 2*

**R95.00**　　£10.00　　US$17.50　　C$25.00　　A$25.00　　NZ$32.50

---

## MAPOLISA – Some Reminiscences of a Rhodesian Policeman
*David Craven*

The author's memoirs of his service in the British South Africa Police (BSAP) 1948-69. Capturing a colonial era as "the winds of change" were blowing across Africa. A delightful account of an ordinary policeman simply getting on with his job.

*"…a very readable story… which needed telling"* – Zimbabwe Independent

*Softback; 222 x 152mm; 216 pages; 66 b/w illustrations, map; 0 620 22522 X Reprinted 2000*

**R100.00**　　£10.00　　US$17.50　　C$25.00　　A$25.00　　NZ$32.50

---

## ONE COMMANDO – Rhodesia's Last Years, the Guerrilla War
*Dick Gledhill*

The author's fictionalized account of his service in the elite parachute battalion, One Commando, the Rhodesian Light Infantry, during the height of the guerrilla war. A cracker of a story; action-packed all the way. Well balanced and intriguing.

*Softback; 178 x 111mm; 218 pages; 20 b/w photographs; 0 646 31036 4 RLI Publishing*

**R100.00**　　£10.00　　US$17.50　　C$25.00　　A$25.00　　NZ$32.50

# CURRENTLY AVAILABLE

## THE ELITE – The Story of the Rhodesian SAS
*Barbara Cole*

The best-selling account of "C" Squadron, the SAS during the Rhodesian bush war of the 1970s. First published in 1985, this book is timeless in content and appeal.

*"…possibly the most important book about the Rhodesian war from the military side"* – Daily Dispatch

*Softback ; 194 x 130mm; 461 pages; 56 b/w photographs, maps; 0 620 08517 7*
*Three Knights Publishing*

**R100.00**   £10.00   US$17.50   C$25.00   A$25.00   NZ$32.50

---

## BUSH HORIZONS – The Story of Aviation in Southern Rhodesia 1896-1940
*Squadron Leader N.V. Phillips*

Edited by Group Captain Bill Sykes, Wing Commander Peter Cooke and Professor Dick Christie. Packed with fascinating accounts of the development of flight in the "early days" in Africa. A unique account that is a must for anyone remotely interested in aviation.

*Softback; 212 x 146mm; 204 pages; 146 b/w illustrations, maps; 0 797 41845 8*
*Air Forces Association; Reprinted 1999*

**R120.00**   £15.00   US$25.00   C$35.00   A$35.00   NZ$45.00

---

## FIRE, FLOOD AND ICE – Search and Rescue Missions of the South African Air Force
*Brigadier Dick Lord*

A compilation of South African search and rescue missions, both military and civil, over the past decade. Foreword by Lieutenant-General Willem Hechter, Chief of the SAAF. Of heartwarming dedication and courage, these true stories will leave the reader breathless.

*Hardback; 228 x155mm; 280 pages; 90 b/w & colour photographs; 6 maps;*
*0 620 22901 2*

**R140.00**   £15.00   US$25.00   C$35.00   A$35.00   NZ$45.00

# CURRENTLY AVAILABLE

## OPEN COCKPIT OVER AFRICA
*Victor Smith*

The intimate account by one of Africa's pioneering aviators, of what it was like to fly open-cockpit, single-engined aircraft the length and breadth of primitive Africa in the 1930s. A breathtaking and thrilling saga of aerial trail-blazing from London to the Cape and back. It is also of the author's experiences as Beaufighter pilot in the Balkan Air Force during World War II.

*"...ranking with the best of Sir Francis Chichester's three books on his air pioneering travels" – Hammond Innes*

*Softback; 229 x 152mm; 196 pages; 58 b/w illustrations; maps, diagrams; 0 798 50773 X; Faircape Books*

**R120.00**   £15.00   US$25.00   C$35.00   A$35.00   NZ$45.00

## HOW WE KEPT THE FLAG FLYING
*Donald Macdonald*

Similar facsimile reprint of 1$^{st}$ Edition, (Ward, Lock & Co. Ltd., 1900). This enduring story of the siege of Ladysmith is the first in our series of Anglo-Boer War titles, commemorating the Anglo-Boer War Centenary 1999-2002. A classic in every sense, and as relevant today as a century ago.

*Hardback; 213 x 137mm; 303 pages; 12 b/w illustrations; 0 620 23342 7 2$^{nd}$ Edition*

**R100.00**   £15.00   US$25.00   C$35.00   A$35.00   NZ$45.00

## HALT! ACTION FRONT! – With Colonel Long at Colenso
*Darrell Hall*

The detailed account of the three batteries of the 4$^{th}$ Brigade Division, Royal Field Artillery (7$^{th}$, 14$^{th}$, and 66$^{th}$), and the six "Long 12s" of the Royal Navy, which operated under the direct command of Colonel C.J. Long RHA, commanding the Artillery of the Natal Field Force, at the Battle of Colenso, on 15$^{th}$ December 1899. These three RFA batteries still serve today in the 26$^{th}$ Field Regiment, Royal Artillery, as now 16$^{th}$, 17$^{th}$ and 159$^{th}$ respectively.

*Hardback; 228 x 155mm; 208 pages; over 100 b/w photographs, diagrams, maps; 0 620 24112 8*

**R100.00**   £15.00   US$25.00   C$35.00   A$35.00   NZ$45.00

# CURRENTLY AVAILABLE

## SOUTH AFRICAN WAR BOOKS – An Illustrated Bibliography
*R.G. Hackett*

Definitive compilation of English language publications relating to the Anglo-Boer War 1899-1902. A masterpiece and already a collector's item, with only 1,200 copies printed.

*"With meticulous regard for detail, this bibliography of contemporary books about the Boer War is a collector's must… a delightful insight into the mind of the bibliophile…"* – Jim Mitchell, The Star

Hardback; 316 x 222mm; 216 pages; Over 200 colour and b/w illustrations; 0 952 00390 2
P.G. de Lotz Military Bookseller

| R850.00 | £65.00 | US$100.00 | C$150.00 | A$150.00 | NZ$195.00 |

## SAND IN THE WIND
*Keith Meadows*

Of wildlife and war, this haunting novel, drawn from factual events and set in the great Zambezi Valley encompasses the fading era of Rhodesia to the dawn of Zimbabwe. Evocatively captures the essence of wild Africa. Following the traditions of Robert Ruark.

*"A land without animals is a dead land"* – Old Shangaan saying

Softback; 220 x 148mm; 522 pages; 0 797 41785 0; Thorntree Press

| R120.00 | £15.00 | US$25.00 | C$35.00 | A$35.00 | NZ$45.00 |

## RUPERT FOTHERGILL – Bridging a Conservation Era
*Keith Meadows*

The full story of Operation Noah and its instigator, world-famous game warden Rupert Fothergill—the reluctant hero. The story of the famous animal rescue from the rising waters of the Kariba Dam on the Zambezi River. Operation Noah was to become the cornerstone of Zimbabwe's progressive conservation policies. With beautiful sketches by renowned wildlife artist Ian Henderson.

Hardback; 214 x 150mm; 264 pages; 40 sepia photographs; 0 797 41608 0; Thorntree Press

| R120.00 | £15.00 | US$25.00 | C$35.00 | A$35.00 | NZ$45.00 |

## WANKIE – The Story of a Great Game Reserve
*Ted Davison*

The enduring account of the birth and development of one of Africa's great game reserves—the Hwange (Wankie) National Park in Zimbabwe—and the legendary ranger who started it all. With the foreword by former prime minister, Ian Douglas Smith.

*"There are some who can live without wild things, and some who cannot"* – Aldo Leopold, A Sand County Almanac

Hardback; 220 x 150mm; 276 pages; 87 sepia illustrations; Sketches, maps; 0 797 41874 1
3$^{rd}$ Impression; Thorntree Press

| R120.00 | £15.00 | US$25.00 | C$35.00 | A$35.00 | NZ$45.00 |

# COMING SOON IN 2000

## ANECDOTES OF THE ANGLO-BOER WAR
*Rob Milne*

An absorbing collection of true stories from the Boer War – some tragic, some light-hearted – but at all times entertaining, bringing humanity to the horror of war.

***April**; Softback; 222 x 152mm; illustrated; 0 620 25439 4*

## CYCLONE BLUES
*Chris Cocks*

The author's first novel after his best-selling nonfiction *Fireforce* and *Survival Course*. Set in present-day Zimbabwe and Mozambique, still suffering from the hangovers of civil war – it is a story of love and tragedy, against the backdrop of political machinations and treachery. It successfully examines inter-racial relationships and attitudes and breathes hope into a troubled sub-continent, struggling with its history, its present and its future.

***May**; Softback; 222 x 152mm; 0 620 25438 6*

## KINKASEKI – One day at a time
*Arthur Titherington*

Taken prisoner at the fall of Singapore, the author was to spend the rest of the war as a slave labourer in the Japanese POW camp at Kinkaseki in Formosa (now Taiwan). A chilling exposé of brutality and cruelty. A true story of survival in the tradition of *Tenko* and *The Bridge on the River Kwai*.

***May**; Softback; 222 x 152 mm; illustrated; $2^{nd}$ Edition; 0 620 25441 6*

## BATTLES OF THE TRANSVAAL
*Various—compiled/edited by Rob Milne*

Several celebrated South African historians and enthusiasts have got together to produce this fascinating compilation of the battles of the Transvaal during the Anglo-Boer War.

***June**; Softback; 222 x 152mm; illustrated; maps; 0 620 25421 1*

## THE MANY HOUSES OF EXILE
*Richard Jurgens*

A fascinating autobiographical account of the author's experiences as an ANC exile. From his conscription into the South African army, to ANC recruitment whilst studying philosophy at Wits University – to life in the ANC camps in Zambia, Tanzania and Zimbabwe – and finally to 8 years exile in Holland. Richard Jurgens is the new voice of South African literature.

***July**; Softback; 222 x 152mm; 0 620 25440 8*

# COMING SOON IN 2000

## THE REGIMENT – A History and the Uniforms of the British South Africa Police

*Dick Hamley*

A stunning coffee-table pictorial production, with the author's own vivid water-colour plates included. Traces the development of this fine police force from the 1890s to 1980. Also a Special leather-bound Edition.

*August; Softback; illustrated; $2^{nd}$ Edition; 0 620 25394 0*

---

## A PRIDE OF EAGLES – The Definitive History of the Rhodesian Air Force 1920-80

*Beryl Salt*

From the arrival of the *Silver Queen* in 1920, through the "Rhodesia squadrons" of World War 2, to the cessation of hostilities after the Rhodesian bush war in 1980, the author has spent over 30 years compiling this comprehensive account of this small, but professional and effective air force. Officially endorsed by the Air Force Associations of Zimbabwe, this book will be prized by lovers of Africana and aviation buffs worldwide. Also a Limited Edition of 75 copies.

*November; Hardback; illustrated; maps/diagrams; 0 620 23759 7*

---

## COVOS-DAY BOOKS

P. O. Box 6996
Weltevredenpark, 1715
South Africa

tel +2711-475 0922
fax +2711-475 8974
email: covos@global.co.za
website at: www.mazoe.com

### UK/Europe Sales and Distribution
## VERULAM PUBLISHING

152a Park Street Lane, Park Street
St Albans, Herts AL2 2AU
tel: +44-1727-872 770
fax +44-1727-873 866
email: verulampub@compuserve.com

# ORDER FORM

☐ Yes, I would like to order

| Title | | | | Quantity | Currency | Total |
|---|---|---|---|---|---|---|
| | | | | | | |
| | | | | | | |
| | | | | | | |
| | | | | | | |
| | | | | | | |
| | | | | | | |
| | | | | | | |
| | | | | Total Postage | | |
| | | | | Total Order | | |

Name..................................................................................................................................

Postal Address..................................................................................................................

..........................................................................................................................................

Postal code...............................Country...........................................................................

Tel .........................................................................(include country/area code)

Fax.........................................................................(include country/ area code)

Email..................................................................................................

**PAYMENT OPTION**

☐ I enclose a cheque/bank draft for the total value of the order

☐ Please charge the amount of ................................................... to my Visa/Master card

    Card no................................................................................................

    Expiry date...........................Last 3 digits on reverse of card........................................

    Signature.................................................................. Date.....................................

**Send your order and payment to:**

Covos-Day Books  
P. O. Box 6996, Weltevredenpark  
1715, South Africa

or fax/email your order and credit card details to:  
fax +2711-475 8974  
email: covos@global.co.za

You may also choose to order via our website at **www.mazoe.com**

**Postage rates per one book**

| Destination | South Africa | UK; Europe | USA; Asia; S.America | Canada | Australia | New Zealand |
|---|---|---|---|---|---|---|
| Surface Mail | R25.00 | £8.50 | $15.00 | C$20.00 | A$20.00 | NZ$25.00 |
| Airmail | n/a | £14.50 | $25.00 | C$35.00 | A$35.00 | NZ$45.00 |

- Rates include postage, packaging and insurance
- Please select either Surface Mail (4-8 weeks delivery) or Airmail (7-10 days delivery) and add the total P & P charges to your order
- For Limited and Special Editions, please double the P & P rates
- For orders of 3 books or more, please deduct 25% off the total P & P costs